©Pastor Hlompho Phamodi
First Published 2015
ISBN: 978-0-620-65742-6

All rights reserved. No part of this publication may be reproduced, stored in a retrieval system or transmitted in any form or by any means, electronically, mechanically, photocopy, recording or otherwise without prior written permission of the publishers.

This book is a publication of
HLOMPHO PHAMODI PUBLICATIONS
Cape Town, Western Cape
South Africa
Email: **hlomph@hotmail.com**
Contact No: +27(0) 21 839 4286 / (+27)0 83 754 1746

Remember to rate this book and sent a review on the book page in
www.Amazon.com
For prayer requests or testimonies, sent us an email on
hlomph@hotmail.com, we will love to hear from you.

Designed and Published by
HLOMPHO PHAMODI PUBLICATIONS

ABOUT THE BOOK

Are you experiencing unexplainable problems, delays, failures, demonic dreams and limitations in your life?

Are you searching for total Deliverance?

Have you ever wondered what Holy Ghost fire prayers are, and their power?

Can a born again Christian be demonized and how?

Then this is the right book for you. This is the day of your deliverance! The Lord has been revealing a lot of truths from His word about the ministry of deliverance. The Church is divided especially with regards to deliverance ministry, as the devils has blinded and mislead Gods people, especially Christians. And many are oppressed by the enemy and not aware of their need for deliverance as they live in denial and ignorance. Deliverance by Fire, by Force will equip you with the truth you need to know and guide you into praying specific targeted prayers from the word of God to help you overcome and be totally delivered from any form of demonic oppression by Fire and by Force in Jesus Name.

ABOUT THE AUTHOR

Pastor Hlompho Phamodi is a born again, chosen vessel of God, a general and a commander in the Kingdom of God, an anointed man of God who is called to proclaim and demonstrate the Word of God. He is called to pastor, coach and equip the saints in the area of Deliverance, Healing and Spiritual warfare. His preaching's and writings are backed up with signs and wonders to deliver, to heal and set free the captives. He is a man under submission to spiritual authority; he serves under the apostolic covering of Apostle M Oliphant at His Grace Family Church in Cape Town. He is a married to 'Makarabo Phamodi and lives in Cape Town South Africa.

DEDICATION & ACKNOWLEDGEMENT

Firstly I will love to dedicate this work to the Most Important Person on this planet and in my life, the Holy Spirit Himself, without Him I can do nothing. Without His fire in my life this are just mere words.

This book is nothing but proof that with God all things are possible. Since accepting Jesus Christ there has been many great mentors and people that God has used and I will love to thank God for every person who contributed to my spiritual life. I am a product of their prayers and service.

To my precious wife 'Makabo Phamodi, your love and prayers continue to inspire me to do more. I am grateful to the Lord for a suitable helper, may God richly bless you.

I have been blessed to have a wonderful spiritual father Apostle Oliphant and mother Mama Oliphant I want to give God all the glory for giving me such parents. The apostolic covering upon my life through my spiritual father has brought so much favor and blessings in my life. This book is an example of what God can do when you meet your ordained spiritual parents and helpers of destiny.

To my amazing parents Mr. and Mrs. Phamodi, who continue to pray for me I give God all the glory for keeping you faithful to end.

To my family in the Lord from His Grace family Church, and Fill the Gap ministries back in Lesotho I bless the Lord for my parents Archbishop M Kolisang and Mama Bishop Kolisang from Fill the Gap Ministries in Lesotho; I am a product of their prayers and teachings.

To countless sons and daughters of the Most High God all over the world who believe that Jesus has come to set the captives free. May your faith grow from strength to strength.

TABLE OF CONTENTS

- ABOUT THE BOOK 2
- ABOUT THE AUTHOR 3
- DEDICATION & ACKNOWLEDGEMENT 4
- INTRODUCTION 9
- **CHAPTER 1** 12
- **WHY DELIVERANCE BY FIRE AND BY FORCE?** 12
  - Why Deliverance? 13
  - What is Deliverance? 14
  - Why by Fire? 15
  - Is He the Holy Ghost or Holy Spirit? 16
  - What about praying Holy Ghost fire prayers? 17
  - So who is the Holy Ghost Fire? 18
  - Prayer is as incense and Fire in the spirit realm 19
  - Prayer, Fire, Deliverance and open heaven 20
  - The power of persistent prayer against the kingdom of darkness 21
  - Why by force? 31
  - Your authority vs the devils authority 32
  - Fasting and Prayer for Chapter 1 34
- **CHAPTER 2** 37
- **THE HOLY GHOST FIRE AND HIS BAPTISM** 37
  - Prophetic Word "Messengers of Fire" 38
  - We need the Fire 40
  - How is the Spirit like Fire and what is His purpose? 40
  - The Fire and Anointing 47
  - Fellowship with the Holy Spirit 49
  - My Holy Ghost and Fire baptism 51
  - Experiencing the Fire in the baptism 53
  - Fasting and Prayer Chapter 2 55
- **CHAPTER 3** 60
- **CAN A CHRISTIAN BE POSSESSED?** 60
  - Possession vs Demonisation 61
  - You were bought back 61
  - You are like a house that is been bought 62
  - Can a Christian have a demon? let's see from the Bible 65

How can an evil spirit and Holy Spirit dwell within the same person at the same time? 66
A Word for the curse breakers 67
Prayers and Fasting Chapter 3 69
CHAPTER 4 70
THREE KINDS OF DEMONIC MANIFESTATION 70
THREE KINDS OF DEMONIC MANIFESTATION 71
What does it mean to be spiritually oppressed? 71
What does it mean to be spiritually obsessed? 73
What does it mean to be spiritually possessed? 75
How demons operate 76
What is the spirits of infirmity and how it operates 77
What are seducing spirits 77
What about unclean spirits 79
How demons gain control 79
CHAPTER 5 82
HOW SATAN FIGHTS CHRISTIANS 82
A meeting from the underworld convention 82
How Satan and his agents attack the Christians 84
How Christians are known by the demons? 87
The making of backslidden Christians 88
Destroying Churches 90
Fasting and Prayer Chapter 5 90
CHAPTER 6 93
DEALING WITH THE MARINE KINGDOM 93
Exposing the kingdom, my personal testimony 93
What are marine spirits 94
Marine spirits in the Bible 95
Why marine spirits are so powerful 97
Startling confessions of a Marine Queen 98
The city under the Sea 100
Our forefathers and Water spirits 104
General features of marine spirits 105
Signs of marine spirits operation 107
Mother of the Water (Mamny Water) 108
How do people get polluted by marine spirits 109

Fasting and Prayer Chapter 6 112
CHAPTER 7 .... **115**
DREAMS AND THEIR ASSIGNMENT **115**
Sources of dreams 115
Types of dreams 116
Causes of demonic dreams 117
Dream robbers attack 118
Loss of spiritual appetite dream attack 119
Spirit of death (untimely death dream attack) 120
Demoting dreams attack 121
Family curses dream attack 122
Financial robbers dream attack 123
Evil monitiring spirits dream attacks 123
Spirit of infirmity (sickness dream attacks) 124
Evil patterns dream attack 124
Spirit of stagnation dream attack 124
How to break demonic dreams 125
CHAPTER 8 .... **127**
DEALING WITH ALTARS & WITCHCRAFT ATTACKS **127**
Different types of altars 128
What are the effects of this altars 130
Dealing with the spirit of witchcraft 132
Who is practicing witchcraft 133
Witchcraft in the church 134
What is witcraft attack? 135
Sucks life out of you 136
Manifestations of the spirit of witchcraft 136
Watch out for controllers 137
CHAPTER 9 .... **139**
RENOUCING MEMBERSHIP OF EVIL ASSOCIATIONS **139**
Renoucing curses: 141
Deliverance prayer from spirit husband or wives: 142
Covenants and yokes breaking prayers: 143
CHAPTER 10 .... **144**
POWER OF MIDNIGHT PRAYER **144**
When is this hour? 144

The power of the midnight prayer 145
Witcraft hour 146
CHAPTER 11 150
MAINTAING YOUR DELIVERANCE 150
Seven steps to mainatain your deliverance 150
How to keep free from oppressing spirits...151
Holding on to your deliverance 152
CHAPTER 12 153
HOW DO I KNOW I NEED DELIVERANCE? 153
The gift of discernment..153

INTRODUCTION

MY PRAYER FOR ALL WHO WILL TOUCH OR READ THIS BOOK;

> *"Father in the Name of Jesus Christ, Holy Ghost Fire of God touch Your sons and daughters now in Jesus name. As they read through these book let them feel your fire and your presence in their spirit, soul and entire body, let the bound be set free, let the sick be healed in Jesus Name. Thank you Lord that whoever reads this words will experience the fire and touch of God that will turn their lives around and wherever this book goes; there, deliverance will go, power will go, healing will go, provision will go, breakthrough will go, no one will read this book and remain the same. Your divine protection and Angelic ministry be with them all, I degree, declare and prophecy upon their lives that they will not only be transformed by these book but that they will be mightily used of God, in the mighty Name of Jesus Christ .Amen."*

A PERSONAL NOTE TO YOU

I want to commend you for picking this book; I want you to know that it is by the Spirit of God that has inspired you to pick it. Prepare yourself to be changed and empowered; prepare to be a different person all together. I can guarantee you that you will feel the presence of God as you go through these pages. You will experience deliverance and freedom in Christ Jesus. As you keep reading, there will be some resistance but, don't be intimidated by the attacks that will come, be committed to the prayers, fasting's and instructions in this book. Do them faithfully and expect God to honor your faith. I wrote this book in period in my life when God was speaking to me about the Apostolic and Prophetic wave of deliverance and fire that was coming upon the Church of Jesus Christ, this anointing will be so powerful that it will set free anyone on its way; be it a devil worshipper, a Satanist, a marine agent, witches and anyone who is bound by the devil, will not escape this anointing. I simply obeyed and I believe you are one of the many that God is raising and appointing under these anointing. The heading says it all it's about deliverance by fire and by force. There will be no negotiations this time. The devil and his agents will have to pack their bags and go. Read this book prayerfully and be violent in the spirit as you pray. It's your season to break loose; for the kingdom of God suffers violence and the violent take it by force. It's never been and will never be a kingdom of word only, but of power. That power is in you and through this book you will know it, and be used powerfully for Gods glory.

God instructed Moses in the wilderness and raised him to go to Egypt and confront Pharaoh who represents a stubborn generational oppression as it is with so many of our people, coming from generations, families or bloodlines that have been oppressed for years by this spirit of Pharaoh. Yes you might be saved but Pharaoh is kept you bound. God instructed Moses, and He is sending me into your life through these book to confront Pharaoh and say; *Pharaoh of your father's house, The Lord God of Israel is saying enough is enough it's time to let My people Go, it's time for their total deliverance by fire by force.*

Declare this prayer three times out loud;
> ➢ *Pharaoh of my father's house, hear the word of the Lord; let me go so that I can worship my God, in Jesus Name.*

That is the divine instruction whether the devil likes it or not he has to free you. It's time to put the devil where he belongs and put Christ in His place. Demons have no place in your life, failure, sickness, poverty and any form of lack or curse has no place in your life. I believe the Lord is called me to share these truths from His word to bring you to total deliverance in every area of your life. I believe the reason why the Lord will have me write this book is due to prophetic words and many dreams and visions that He showed me and confirmed them that I am called into the ministry of deliverance. I am not trying to repeat what has been done or written but I believe there is an anointing upon my life and it's a specific anointing that will impact your life in a significant way especially in area of total deliverance. The Lord is ready to minister to you. Be blessed as you read. **If you are not born-again please accept Jesus Christ as your Lord and savior now before you go any further. Pray these words out loud;**

'Lord Jesus forgive me of my sins, I confess with my mouth that Jesus Christ is Lord and believe in my heart that God raised Him from the dead, I accept you Jesus, come and live in my heart. In Jesus name I pray. Amen.'

If you are already born again, depart from any form of sin, live a holy life, be in submission to God and spiritual authority and let God do the rest.

May you experience Him like never before. I am praying daily for you and I believe God will always come through. Expect a breakthrough. Our email and contacts are at the beginning of this book. Join the many conquerors (messengers of fire) that are testifying daily of what the Lord is done, sent us your testimonies and prayer requests.

Pastor Hlompho Phamodi
His Grace Family Church, Cape Town
April 2015

CHAPTER 1

WHY DELIVERANCE BY FIRE AND BY FORCE?

Without wasting your time with long speeches and vain words I want get straight to the point, the devil is a liar, you will be totally free by Fire and by Force in Jesus Mighty name. Yes it sound like a popular saying, perhaps you have heard it so many times and got so used to it. Perhaps you have a different approach to deliverance or don't see the point of saying all this statements. But the Prophet Obadiah said it so well in Obadiah 1: 17 that;

Upon mount Zion there shall be deliverance and holiness and the house of Jacob shall possess their possession, the house of Jacob shall be a fire and house of Joseph the flame...

Are you a Child of God? Then you belong to mount Zion, are you of the house of Jacob? Then you are a flame of fire.

Let me start by saying if you are well and on your mountain top having no need to get your promised victories, breakthroughs or blessings in this life then you don't have to read this book. This book is for people that are ready to go to the enemies camp and to take back what belongs to them by the Power of the Holy Ghost in His raging Fire and by Force, because the devil is not going to fold his arms while you come for your stuff.

DO YOU WANT YOU ABUNDANT LIFE?

Let's go down together and with the Lord the Man of war go and take our riches, our health our breakthrough our sons and daughters. You are His battle Axe; you are the weapon of war; with you the Lord says; I will break nations in pieces; with you I will destroy kingdoms; with you I will break in pieces man and woman. It's going to take you and Him together in this one (Jeremiah 51:20-23). He needs you and me to go down and take our things back to their rightful place. I am about to take you on a journey that will turn your test to a testimony, your mess into a message. You have been a victim for too long it's time to taste victory. You have been in a storm it's time for your peace, it's time for your shame to turn to fame, your sickness to healing, your poverty to prosperity, your story to glory in Jesus Name. It's time to say bye! bye! to sickness, poverty, failure, curses and hallow! to blessings, to divine health, to freedom in Christ, to victory and financial freedom.

IT'S ALL ABOUT FAITH AND WORKS

I once took two chairs in my house and called meeting to all in the house I addressed everyone including poverty and sickness whom I brought two chairs for I then said to everyone; that I have an announcement to make, I looked straight to the two chairs and said poverty and sickness you are not paying rent in this house now I am chasing you out of my house in Jesus name. I opened the door and commanded them to leave. And praise God they never returned since.

WHY DELIVERANCE?

The word Deliverance is been wrongly understood or interpreted, Deliverance is not a show of demons versus the man of God, deliverance is not demons speaking and people falling on the ground, Deliverance in not vomiting or shaking uncontrollably. Deliverance is not some new doctrine in the church and absent of the Love of God or Christian ethics and doctrines. Deliverance is the very Spirit of God. The Bible declares where the Spirit of the Lord is there is liberty. Jesus ministry was Deliverance He cast out demons and healed the sick. If Jesus had a church in our todays language or a ministry. He will be dealing with demons and setting people free. He would teach them and deliver them. I don't see Him giving long seminary theological teachings and being ceremonious. No! He will out of His love for you and me make sure that the blind see, the poor are fed and delivered, the dead are raised to life, the bound loosed and the lost found. He will put the third person of trinity to work He is called the Holy Ghost. He comes in power and brings you and me to total victory, deliverance and sanctification. He does this so that we can be soldiers of Christ to take back what the devil is stolen and exercise His dominion in the earth.

WHAT IS DELIVERANCE?

Deliverance is a word derived from the Word Salvation. Salvation is not only to be forgiven of your sins.no! It's more than that Jesus didn't die so that your sins are forgiven only but He came that you might have life and life to the full. In the gospel when Jesus used the word salvation; like in Luke 19:9

Jesus said to him today salvation has come to this house because he also is a son of Abraham. He used the Greek word *Soteria* which is the Greek word for Salvation and that includes the following; **Deliverance, Healing, Restoration and Forgiveness of sins**. When the Bible speaks of being saved, the Greek word *sozo* it refers to being forgiven, being delivered being restored, being healed and being provided for. It's for the total man; spirit soul and body.

Salvation is a present possession of Gods abundant life and blessings with the full realization of your eternal life.
Say this out loud and clear;

> ➤ I declare that every lie tying me down from total victory be consumed by the fire of the Holy Ghost in Jesus Name.
> ➤ I declare that I am receiving my full benefits of my salvation now in Jesus Name.

Some of us experience a measure of freedom and think that is enough. Yes you love God you are saved but you are not progressing, you are in debts and all kinds of challenges hinder you from fully enjoying your life. You need this knowledge. Christ didn't save you to be a laughing stock, enough is enough if you truly love God and have His Spirit in you, total deliverance is your portion. All of salvation and its benefits are yours in Jesus name.

WHY BY FIRE?

Years ago when I received the baptism of the Holy Ghost. I will use the word Holy Ghost and Holy Spirit interchangeably. When I was baptized in the Holy Spirit for the first time I remember the Lord spoke to me about these promise and I specifically remember His promise through John in Matthew 3:11 that says;

*I indeed baptize you with water unto repentance, but he who is coming after me is mightier than I whose sandals I am not worthy to carry. He will baptize you with the **Holy Spirit and fire**.*

Since then for a long time after my Holy Ghost baptism I tried to find out if I was baptized in the Holy Spirit alone or in fire alone or in both. It felt like there wasn't enough explanation on this subject so I searched the scriptures, prayed and kept enquiring. It appeared to me that there is one baptism as fulfilled in Acts 2:1 -3 and it is the baptism of the Holy Spirit and Fire. It's one experience. There should not be a confusion regarding this matter no way in the Bible are we told of two baptisms of the Holy Ghost, one for the Holy ghost alone and one for fire. There is only one, even if it repeats itself like in Acts 4:31 but its same Holy Spirit and fire.

So why by Fire? God answers by fire (1Kings 18:24), His fire is a Weapon used against His enemies to destroy them (see Deuteronomy 9:3). There is nothing wrong in praying down the fire of God, and likely so there is nothing wrong in associating fire with the Holy Ghost, because the Spirit of God moves in fire, weather of judgment or sanctification or destruction it is still the divine fire of God. That is why 1Thessanolians 5:19 the Bible say Do not quench the Spirit fire. **The fire of God should be used and it's very powerful in the spiritual realm.** One of the names of the Holy Spirit is called Spirit of burning in Isaiah 4;4 Let me give you an example to explain my point; for example a woman to her husband is his wife but to somebody she is just a woman, so it is with the Holy Spirit same Person but different names and functions.

In deliverance ministry or spiritual warfare, fire is a mighty Weapon and it is used to devour or consume the enemies of God we use fire with the Holy Ghost. **It is like sending the Power of God (the Holy Spirit) in his destruction force (fire) in the Name of the Lord (Jesus Christ).** In other words the force of God that we release is the Holy Ghost fire of God. And it's used mostly in deliverance. He remains the Person of the Holy Ghost but he takes a form of fire.

In several occasions we have prayed for people and whenever the Holy Ghost fire was called people began to feel literally fire upon them as the demons in the spirit can see this fire and it's an all-consuming fire of God that destroys His enemies.

In other words you cannot separate God from fire because **He is a consuming fire (Hebrews 12:29)** you can't separate the Holy Spirit who is God and the Power of God from fire. God has weapons in His word such as the Blood of Jesus, the Name of Jesus etc. The fire of God is one of the weapons that God uses in the power of the Holy Ghost in Jesus Name. **The same way you can use the Name of Jesus as a weapon or a spiritual force you can also use the Holy Ghost fire as a weapon or a force against forces of darkness.** I recommend that deliverance ministers be well taught and trained in this area. Most importantly to follow the leading of the Holy Ghost as it's not about calling down fire but being in tune with the Spirit of God because **we don't use Him He use us, We don't possess the Holy Spirit, but the Spirit possess us**. God uses different methods and ways so remain tuned and obedient to Him.

IS HE THE HOLY GHOST OR HOLY SPIRIT?

Let me clarify this now so you understand, firstly I want to address the issue of the Holy Ghost and Holy Spirit, yes the original king James version uses the word Holy Ghost and scholars have argued that it is a wrong translation. Because they say Ghost means departed dead spirit. Now I want you to rest assured and I know God is the one who knows everything. No matter your theology on this one; the Bible say if we ask God the Father for the Holy Spirit or Holy Ghost whatever one suits you, He will give us what we ask for from our hearts according to Luke 11:13. If you are His son He will give you the Third Person of Trinity. Weather you call Him Holy Ghost or Holy Spirit. See what He says in Luke 11:9-13. God is a perfect God and yes we should use His word in excellence but God won't give you another spirit if you ask Him for what you have come to except as the Name of God, the Holy Ghost or Holy Spirit. So rest assured you will know when He comes He responds to your heart he response to His word.

Let me give you a real life story; a friend of mine was once attacked by robbers. He was a born again child of God and it was one of those unfortunate experiences that he was at the wrong place at the wrong time. It so happen as he was making his way into a library in the middle of the day two young men approached him and took out two big knives. He was terrified as they held him and demanded his cellphone. He said he saw himself on the ground and this was his prayer 'God help me'; as he held his head up high. Guess what; God Almighty intervened according to him they could have stabbed him but God was there instantly to save him. God helped him and he escaped unharmed.

Now when my friend went on his knees and called on God, take note he didn't mention Jesus he said 'God'. There are many gods out there how did heaven know he was referring to the God of Abraham, Isaac and Jacob? And the answer is through his faith in His God and his hearts prayer. So don't be fooled God Knows when you calling Him whether you call on the Holy Ghost or Holy Spirit, the Third person of trinity will show up. It's all about your heart, faith and the direction of that faith.

WHAT ABOUT PRAYING HOLY GHOST FIRE PRAYERS?

Let's talk about praying Holy Ghost Fire prayers here I want to be clear and straight forward. Jesus Name is a weapon, if you can use it in prayer why can't we use the Holy Ghost and fire. There is nothing wrong whatsoever in my own opinion as long as we understand what we doing. **We don't use fire of God on people or our enemies it's meant for the spiritual realm**. Jesus taught against calling down fire on people (Luke 9:54-55). James and John will tell you about this one. Remember we don't fight against flesh and blood. Holy Spirit, Gods fire or Fire Holy Ghost will respond as Jesus Name will respond to whatever **we asking in His name and His will**. So be free child of God. We have different callings as individuals, ministries and churches and let's not condemn those that don't pray like us. We are all called to different functions. Holy Ghost fire is one of the weapons in deliverance ministry and we should be skilled by the Holy Ghost on how to use the fire of the Spirit. We should in fact be led by Him in every prayer or ministry we do. I want you to take note that **I always add; in Jesus Name,** because we are to pray in His Name at all times. Jesus Christ of Nazareth that is the Name that has been raised above all names and when we say it devils tremble, every knee in heaven and on earth and under the earth has to bow to that Name. Demons bow, sickness bow, witches bow, poverty bow, all demonic oppression bow.

WHATEVER YOU DO NEVER MISS THIS NAME, WE TAKE AUTHOURITY AND GET RESULTS WHEN WE PRAY IN THE NAME OF JESUS CHRIST. ALL PRAYER IS DONE IN HIS NAME.

SO WHO IS THE HOLY GHOST FIRE?

The Holy Ghost Fire or Fire of God is the Third Person of Trinity called God the Holy Spirit. He is the divine Presence of God to consume as fire will consume substance or matter. He is **the all-consuming Fire of God**. I will speak more in details about the Fire of God in the next Chapter. **He is God the Holy Spirit at war to combat stubborn enemies of Gods people. In Deuteronomy 9:3 the Word of the Lord declares**

Understand therefore this day that the Lord thy God is he which goes before you; ***as a consuming fire*** *He shall destroy them and shall bring them down before your face; so shalt you drive them out and destroy them quickly, as the Lord has said unto thee.*

Hebrews 12:29 declares ...*For our God is* ***a consuming fire****.*
Declare these prayers three times out loud (each prayer x3);

> ➤ *Father let the Holy Spirit fill me afresh.*
> ➤ *Holy Ghost fire come and burn away every chaff in me in the name of Jesus.*

- ➢ I command every evil plantation in my life come out now by fire with all your roots in the Name of Jesus.
- ➢ I cut myself from every Antichrist spirit and every spirit from………………… (mention the place of your birth) in the name of Jesus.
- ➢ Let all negative fluids and materials circulating in my blood stream be evacuated by fire in Jesus Name.
- ➢ Holy Ghost fire let your fire destroy all my enemies of progress in Jesus Name.

PRAYER IS AS INCENSE AND FIRE IN THE SPIRIT REALM

There is very powerful testimony under this sub-title above that has changed my life especially in the area of spiritual combat or spiritual warfare. It will help you to see how the fire of God operates when we pray; it will open your eyes to the spiritual war that exists in the spirit world. I searched its validity in the scriptures and I was able to qualify it. But let's talk about Prayer, fire and incense first. **Prayer is more than just words or sounds; prayer is literally incense and fire in the realm of the spirit**. Its smoke and fire, it devours it releases a fragrance it's a very powerful weapon we have. When used properly it changes lives, destinies and paralyses the enemy. The devil cannot withstand persistent Spirit filled prayers. God himself cannot help but respond. **The heart of prayer is a key to a delivered life**; it is the source of victory. Let me qualify my statements Psalm 141: 2 says the following;

Let my prayers be set before You as incense, The lifting up of my hands as the evening sacrifice.

Have you ever wondered why God would use incense to symbolize our prayers? I don't know how familiar you are with incense but I want mention a few things about it. Incense is a sweet aromatic stone like a block. It releases a sweet fragrance and it's used mostly for religious purposes. In our case it was God ordinance that God gave to Moses that he was to take sweet spices to make incense compound, he was instructed to put some of it before the testimony in the tabernacle of meeting where God will meet with him. He said it shall be most holy. (Exodus 30:34)

That is exactly what prayer is. It is sweet; it brings a sweet aroma and not a bitter one before the Lord. Hence it's a pleasure to God when we worship and pray. His pleasure releases His blessing. You want to pleasure Him give Him some incense. Now guess; what do you use in order for incense to release its aroma? Fire, yes! You use fire. No fire no aroma. **When we pray, filled with the fire of His Spirit our prayers releases a fragrance that rises to the heavens and pleases our God. This aroma it's a powerful aroma against the evil kingdoms and barriers and the more we burn the incense the more power and open heavens we have.**

The Bible says when Solomon finished praying in 2 Chronicles 7:1 Fire came down from heaven and burnt the offering and sacrifice and the glory the Lord filled the temple. **God is waiting for His living holy sacrifices to raise up a fired incense that will invoke him to bring down His fire.**
Pray this prayer from your heart:
- ➢ Lord may my prayers be as sweet fragrance before you.
- ➢ May the words in my mouth and the meditation in my heart be pleasing to you O Lord.

PRAYER, FIRE, DELIVERANCE AND OPEN HEAVEN

This is why we say deliverance by Fire, We literally raining the Holy Ghost all-consuming Fire of God upon the kingdom of darkness. The devil worshipers and agents of darkness knows this fire very well, they have kept your prayer life limited and yes there is power in prayer and all prayer done in the name of the Lord will shake demons and bring deliverance but I want in this book to introduce you to **THE FIRE OF GOD**, you will feel it burn in your bones, it's the kind that makes you uncomfortable for ordinary Christianity. Jeremiah said His word was like fire shut up in my bones I am weary of holding it I can't contain it. **You can never be ordinary or normal when you encounter the Fire of God.** You will cause witches and demons to scatter, you will not be able to dream demons playing on your mind and cursing you. You will become a thread to the kingdom of darkness. You will become an atomic bomb to their assemblies and meetings. Your prayers will prevail all the time.

THE POWER OF PERSISTENT PRAYER AGAINST THE KINGDOM OF DARKNESS

(Here is the story I promised you)

I remember a story of a devil worshipper who was arrested by the prayers of the saints the story was told by John Mulinde and this is what he said;

I would like to share with you part of a testimony of a saved person who once served the devil. When I heard him give his testimony it so challenged me I did not want to believe it. I had to fast before the Lord for ten days, asking Him, "Lord, is this true?" It was at that time the Lord began to teach me the things that take place in the spiritual realm when we pray.
This man was born after his parents had dedicated him to Lucifer. When he was still in the womb, they performed many rituals to dedicate him to the service of Lucifer. When he was four years old, he began to exercise his spiritual power, and his parents began to fear him. When he was six years old, his father brought him to some witches for them to train him. And by the time he was ten years old, he was doing tremendous exploits for the kingdom of the devil. He was feared by the common witches.

He was still a young boy, but he was so terrible in the things he did. He grew to be a young man in his twenties with a lot of blood on his hands. He killed at will. He had the ability to leave his body through transcendental meditation. And he could levitate; at times his body would rise off the ground and hang in midair. Sometimes he would go into a trance and leave his body; his body would remain behind while he went out into the world, by a practice called "astral-travelling." He was used by Satan to destroy and divide many churches, and to ruin many pastors.

One day, he was assigned to destroy a church that was full of prayer. There had been much division in this church, and much confusion. He began to work against it, but at that time, the pastor called a fast for the whole church. As the church began to fast, there was much repentance and a lot of reconciliation. The people came together and began to pray for the Lord to work in their midst. They continued interceding and crying out to God to have mercy on them and to intervene in their lives. As the days went by, the man came again and again against the church with demon spirits. But a word of prophecy came forth telling the Christians to rise up and wage warfare against the powers of darkness that were attacking the church.

So one day, the man left his body in his room to go astral-travelling. He led a powerful force of demonic spirits against the church. Now this is his testimony: His spirit moved through the air over the church and tried to attack it, but there was a covering of light over the church. Suddenly, an army of angels attacked them and fought against them in the air. All the demons fled, but he was arrested by the angels.

Yes, arrested by the angels! He found himself being held by about six angels. They brought him through the roof right before the church altar. He just appeared there as the people were praying. They were deep in prayer, engaged in spiritual warfare, binding and breaking and casting out. The pastor was on the platform leading the prayers and the warfare. The Spirit of the Lord spoke to the pastor, "The yoke has been broken, and the victim is there before you. Help him through deliverance." As the pastor opened his eyes, he saw the young man lying there. His body was with him; he was in his body. The young man said that he doesn't know how his body joined him; he had left it back in his house. But there he was in his body. He didn't know how he had entered it; all he knew was that the angel had carried him through the roof.

Now these things are difficult to believe. The pastor silenced the church and told them what the Lord had spoken to him, and then asked the young man, "Who are you?" The young man was trembling as the demons began coming out of him. So they prayed for his deliverance, and afterwards he began to share his story. The young man has now come to the Lord, and is an evangelist preaching the gospel. He is being used by the Lord mightily in setting other people free through deliverance.

One night, I (John Mulinde) went to a dinner. The only reason I went was that someone had told me about this young man and I was very curious to see him and to find out if his story was true. So I attended the dinner, and in the evening he was given the chance to give his testimony. He spoke about so many

things. At times he cried because of the things he had done. As he finished, he made an appeal.
There were many pastors in the room. He said, "I appeal to you, pastors. Please teach the people how to pray." The people who don't pray can be taken in anything, in anything by the devil, and there are ways that the enemy can exploit their lives and their prayers. The enemy knows even how to exploit the prayers of those who don't know how to pray. "Teach the people how to use the spiritual armor that God provides."

Then he shared how he led expeditions through the air. He would go with other satanic agents and many demon spirits. It was as if they were working a shift, in the same way that you've got to go and work your shift. He had a regular, time that he was required to go and wage war in the heavenlies. He said that in the heavenlies, in the spiritual realm, if the land is covered by a blanket of darkness, the blanket is so dense it is like solid rock. And it covers the whole area. The spirits are able to go on top of and below the blanket and from there influence the events on earth.

When the evil spirits and human satanic agents finish their shifts, they go down to earth at the points of covenant, on water or on land, to refresh their spirits. How do they refresh their spirits? By the sacrifices that people give at these altars. They could be sacrifices in open witchcraft, sacrifices in bloodshed of all types, including abortion, warfare, and human and animal sacrifices. They could be sacrifices of sexual immorality, in which people practice sexual perversions and all kinds of promiscuity. Such acts strengthen these powers. There are many different types of sacrifices.

He said that when satanic agents are up in the heavenly realm, and Christians begin to pray on earth, the Christians' prayers appear to them in three forms. **All prayers appear like smoke that is rising toward heaven.**

Some prayers appear like smoke that drifts along and vanishes in the air. These prayers come from people who have sin in their lives that they are not willing to deal with. Their prayers are very weak; they are blown away and disappear in the air.

Another type of prayer is also like smoke. It rises upward until it reaches the rock; it cannot break through the rock. These prayers usually come from people who try to purify themselves, but who lack faith as they pray. They usually ignore the other important aspects that are needed when someone prays.

The third type of prayer is like smoke that is filled with fire. *As it rises upward, it is so hot that when it reaches the rock, the rock begins to melt like wax. It pierces the rock and goes through.*

Many times, as people begin to pray, their prayers look like the first type. But as they continue praying, their prayers change and become like the second type of prayer. And as they continue praying, suddenly their prayers ignite into flames. Their prayers become so powerful that they pierce through the rock.

Many times evil agents would notice that prayers were changing and coming very close to becoming fire. These agents would then communicate with other spirits on earth and tell them, "Distract that person from prayer. Stop them from praying. Pull them out."

Many times Christians yield to these distractions. They are pressing through, repenting and allowing the Word to check their spirit. Their faith is growing. Their prayers are becoming more focused. Then the devil notices that their prayers are gaining strength, and the distractions begin. Telephones ring. Sometimes, in the middle of very, very intense prayer, the telephone rings and you think you can go answer it and then come back and continue praying. However, when you return, you go back to the beginning. And that's what the devil wants.

Other kinds of distractions come your way. They may touch your body, bringing pain somewhere. They may make you hungry, causing you to want to go to the kitchen to prepare something to eat. As long as they can get you out of that place, they have defeated you. He said to the pastors, "Teach the people to set aside some time, not just for some casual praying, they can do that the rest of the day. Once a day, they should have a time when they are focusing wholeheartedly on God, without any distractions.

If the people persist in this kind of prayer and allow themselves to be inspired in the spirit and to keep going, something happens in the spirit. The fire touches that rock, and it melts. *The man said that when the melting begins, it is so hot that no demon spirit can stand it. No human spirit can stand it. They all flee. They all run away.*

There comes an opening in the spiritual realm. As soon as it appears, all this trouble in prayer stops. ***The person who is praying on the ground feels like their prayer has suddenly become so smooth, so enjoyable, so powerful and intense.*** *I've discovered that at that moment, we normally lose all awareness of time and other things. Not that we become disorderly; God takes care of our time. But it is as if you lay down everything, and hook up with God. The man said that when the prayers break through, from that moment on there is no resistance at all, and the person praying can continue as long as he wants.* ***There is no resistance to stop him.***

Then he said that after the person finishes praying, the hole remains open. He said that when people rise from their place of prayer, and move on, the open hole moves along with them. They are no longer operating under the blanket. They are operating under an open heaven. He said that in that state, the devil cannot do what he wants against them. The presence of the Lord is like a pillar from heaven resting on their lives. They are protected, and there is so much power inside the pillar that as they move around, the presence touches other people as well. It discerns what the enemy has done in other people. And as they talk to people who are standing with them, they too come inside the pillar. ***As long as they stay inside the pillar, all the bondages placed on them by the enemy weaken.***

So when people who have experienced this spiritual breakthrough share Jesus Christ with sinners, the sinners' resistance is low. It is very easy to bring them through to salvation. When they pray for the sick or pray about other things, the presence that is with them makes all the difference. The man said that the devil hates such people. He said that in places where prayer regularly breaks through in this way, the presence comes upon that place and does not leave.

When people who don't know God enter such a place, all their bondages even suddenly weaken.

If someone is willing to minister to them with patience and love, they could easily be pulled through to salvation, not by power nor by might but by the Spirit of God, Who is present. But he said that if no one bothers to reach out to them, they merely come into His presence, feel convicted, and begin to debate whether or not to yield. If they are not pulled through to salvation, when they walk away from that place, their bondages become stronger. And the devil tries his best to prevent them from entering such an environment again.

As you can imagine, we all sat staring at the man as he told us the things he used to do and see. Then he told us what they would do to those who broke through in prayer. He said that they marked such people and studied them. They would dig up everything they could find about them, so they knew their weaknesses. **When someone overcame them in prayer and broke through, they would communicate with other spirits saying, "Target him with this and this and this.** They are his weaknesses." So when the person walks out of his prayer closet, the spirit of prayer is upon him, the presence is with him, his spirit is high, and the joy of the Lord is his strength. However, as he goes the enemy tries to bring things that can distract him from focusing on the Lord.

If his weakness is in the area of his temper, the enemy will cause people to do things to make him angry. If he is not sensitive to the Holy Spirit, and he allows himself to lose his temper, he takes his eyes off the Lord. He gets angry; he feels furious. Then after a few minutes, he wants to put it behind him and move forward in the joy of the Lord; however, he doesn't feel joyful anymore. He tries to feel good again, but can't. Why? While he was yielding to the temptation, they were working hard to close the opening above him. Once they have restored the rock, the presence is cut off. The person does not cease being a child of God. But the extra anointing on his life, the presence that worked apart from his own effort, is cut off. They seek to know his areas of weakness.

If his weakness is temptation to commit sexual immorality, the enemy will prepare people or events, something to suddenly arouse his passion to move *towards the temptation. And if the man yields to the temptation and opens his mind to receive and entertain its thoughts, when he is through and wants to again move in the anointing, he discovers it is no longer there. You might say, "That's not fair!" Just remember what the Bible says, "Put on the helmet of salvation. Put on the breastplate of righteousness. "We normally do not understand the part these weapons play in warfare. But remember what Jesus told us to pray towards the end of the Lord's Prayer, "Lead us not into temptation, but deliver us from the evil one."*

Every time after you have a breakthrough in prayer, remember you are still a weak human being. Remember you have not yet been made perfect. Say to the Lord, "Lord, I've enjoyed this time of prayer, but as I walk out into the world, lead me not into temptation. Don't allow me to walk into the devil's trap. I know the enemy is setting a trap out there. I don't know what form it is going to take, and I know I am still weak in certain areas. Given the right circumstances, I will yield to temptation. Protect me, Lord. When you see me turning the corner where the trap has been set, cause me to turn the other way. Intervene, O Lord. Don't let me move in only my own strength and ability. Deliver me from the evil one."

God is able to do it. He is able. That is why things happen sometimes. All you need to say is, "Thank you, Jesus." That is why the Apostle Paul wrote in the book of First Thessalonians, "Thank God in everything, for that is the will of God in Christ for you." (1 Thessalonians: 18) Some things are not good. They are painful, and we wonder why God allows them. But if we only knew what He is saving us from, we would thank Him. When we have learned to trust the Lord, we thank Him in everything.

Beloved, I don't know if I should go deeper, because I do not want to start something I cannot finish. But let me just try to go one step further. The man said that when prayer breaks through like that, the answer will always come. He said he did not know of a single case in which prayer broke through and the answer did not come. He said that the answer always came, but that in most cases, it never reached the person who asked for it. Why? The battle in the heavenlies. He said that after they succeeded in cutting off the open heaven and restoring the rock, they would watch the person and wait because they knew the answer would definitely come.

Then the man said something that really shook my faith. It was because of what he shared next that I fasted for ten days asking, "Lord, is this true? Can You prove it to me?" The man said that every Christian has an angel who serves them. Now we know the Bible says that angels are ministering spirits who minister to us. He said that when people pray, the answer comes in the hands of their angel. The angel brings the answer, just like we read in the book of Daniel. Then he said something that was difficult to receive: **If the one who prays knows of the spiritual armor and is clothed with it, the answer comes by an angel who is also clothed in full armor.**

However, if the one who prays doesn't care about being clothed in spiritual armor, their angel comes to them without spiritual armor. **When Christians are careless about the kinds of thoughts that enter their minds and does not fight the battle for their minds, their angels come to them without helmets.** *Whatever spiritual weapon you ignore on earth, your angel does not have it when he serves you.* **In other words, our spiritual armor is not protecting our physical bodies; it is protecting our spiritual exploits.**

The man said that as the angel was coming they would watch him to find the areas that were uncovered, and then attack those areas. If he didn't have a helmet, they would shoot at his head. If he didn't have a breastplate, they would shoot at his chest. If he didn't have shoes, they would make a fire, causing him to have to walk through fire. Now, I am just repeating what the man said. Actually, we asked him, "Can angels feel fire?" You know what his reply was? Remember this is the spiritual realm. They are spirits dealing with spirits. The battle is intense. When they overpower an angel of God, the first thing they go after is the answer he is carrying, and they get it from him. They then give it to people who are involved in cults or witchcraft, so people might say, "I got this because of witchcraft. "Remember what the Bible says in the book of James? All good things come from God. So where does the devil get the things he gives to his people? Some people who cannot have children go to witch doctors and Satanists and become pregnant! Who gave them the baby? Is Satan a creator? No! He steals from those who don't pray through to the end. Jesus said, "Pray without ceasing."(1 Thessalonians 5:17) And then He said, "But when the Son of

Man comes, will He find faith?" (Luke 18:8) Will He find you still waiting? Or will you have given up, and the enemy stolen what you prayed for?

Then the man said that they were not satisfied with just stealing the answer. They were also interested in detaining the angel. They would start fighting against him. And he said that sometimes they would succeed in holding and binding the angel. He said that when that happens, the Christian on earth becomes a victim as well. **They can do anything to that Christian because he is left totally without ministry in the spiritual realm.**

I asked him, "Do you mean that an angel can be held captive by demonic forces?" The man did not know the Scriptures at the time he was saying all this. He did not know very many verses. He was just sharing his experience. He said that they could not hold the angel very long because as other Christians prayed elsewhere, reinforcements would come and the angels would go free. However, if the Christian responsible did not pray through, he remained a captive. **Then the enemy would send his own angel to them as an angel of light. That is how deception comes—false visions and false prophecies, false leading or guidance in the spirit, and the making of all kinds' of wrong decisions.** *And many times this person is open to all kinds of attacks and bondages.*

And I asked the Lord. I left that dinner extremely troubled. I said, "Lord, I don't want to even try to believe this." It takes away all of my confidence, my security. During the ten days that I sought the Lord, the Lord did two things: He not only confirmed the things I had heard, He also opened my mind to understand a lot more of what happens in the spiritual realm that the man could not tell us. And two, He led me to see what we are supposed to do as the things are happening so that we are not defeated, but can overcome. We need to know and really come to terms with three things.

First: How to use the weapons of our warfare. The Bible calls them the armor of God. It is not our armor; it is God's armor. When we use it, we allow God to fight on our behalf. Second: Understand the relationship between ministering spirits—angels—and our spiritual lives, and be sensitive to what is happening in our hearts as a leading regarding what needs to be done in the spiritual realm on our behalf. That brings us to the third thing: The Holy Spirit. **We** *should not regard the Holy Spirit as our servant, who is serving us and bringing us things. He does not run back and forth between us and the Father to tell Him what we need.* That is the angels' job. He stands by our side. Doing what? Guiding us, teaching us, leading us and helping us to pray in the right way. And when these things are happening in the spiritual realm, He lets us know. Sometimes He wakes you up in the middle of the night and says, "Pray." But you say, "No! My time has not yet come." And He says, "Pray now!" Why? He sees what is happening in the spiritual realm. Sometimes He says, "Fast tomorrow!" But you say, "Oh, no; I'll start on Monday!"

But He understands what is happening in the spiritual realm. We should learn to be sensitive to the Holy Spirit. He guides us in paths of righteousness. The battle is not ours; the battle is the Lord's! Hallelujah! We can overcome! There is enough power to overcome! Jesus has already finished the work. We should not lose. There is enough grace, enough power, for victory.

This story has altered my spiritual life in an amazing way, I have never been the same since and I pray that such stories and many others like this one, together with the prayers and the knowledge that you will get from reading this book that your life will change for the better. We overcome by the blood of the Lamb and by the word of our testimony. It's time to persist in prayer; it's time to fight for an open heaven. May God grand you the grace to pray till your breakthrough in Jesus name I pray. Amen.

Are you looking for a demon chasing, Holy Ghost Fire filled life? Get in touch with the Fire of God and your life will never be the same again. As you can hear from this story it's the power of persistent violent prayers with the amour of God and His righteousness covering us and working in our favor that we can live in an open heaven. That's what I call supernatural living.

Say this prayer seven hot times until you feel a release;
Every demonic spirit hindering my answered prayers I bind you now by Fire in Jesus Mighty name;

> ➢ *Loose my Angle*
> ➢ *Loose my breakthrough*
> ➢ *Loose my Provision*

> *Loose my Healing*
> *Loose my finances*
> *Loose my gifts*
> *Loose my family*

WHY BY FORCE?

It's quite clear that demons are stubborn; they have what I call illegal rights and feel like no one can move them. But they don't have a right over your life unless you give them. Make sure you read the section in chapter three where I speak about open doors. **The enemy gains access and rights upon your life based on the open doors that you allow him to use.**

The kingdom of God suffers violence and the violent take it by force. **Life doesn't give you what you deserve, but it gives you what you fight for.** Right throughout the Bible God used people that we willing to come out of their comfort zone. There is no such thing as; sit down and your answers will come, no! We are commanded to fight and the Bible calls us soldiers in 2 Timothy 2:4. Deliverance is a strenuous and a very militant ministry, the demons are stubborn and territorial. We can't afford to be casual and nice to them. So be aggressive on them and they will go.

Whenever you pray for a person to be delivered remember you are not dealing with the person but the spirit in them. So yes we are moved with compassion as we minister but we have to forcefully exercise our authority. God is a Man of War Yes we call Him Prince of Peace but He is a militant God. You and I have His DNA as a born again children of God so you have to be militant. **The amour of God was never meant for our defense but was meant for offence. The best method of war is offence; don't wait till the devil knocks at your door keep him running at all times. Make a point that you are ahead of him.**

We are at war and victory is ours but we must take it by force. There is times when God had lead me into militant prayers and prophetic actions I can remember the time I was so down and out, very depressed and having no hope, I pitied myself over and over but it didn't help; until God spoke to me to go to the beach and to shout out loud as I prayed. I obeyed; it wasn't easy but I dragged myself to the beach and as I began to pray the Lord kept strengthening me. I could have given up, but the little strength I still had in me when I used it. It broke the spirit of depression just like that. Deliverance is by force period, and sometimes when there is no one to pray for us we have to strengthen ourselves in the Lord. Like David when he was coming back to Ziklag and found it burned and his wives and whole community taken captive. The Bible says, the men who were with him spoke of stoning him, but David chose to strengthen himself in the Lord, he used force to lift himself up and God said to him David fight back for you shall doubtless recover all. See story in 1Samuel 30.

Deliverance by force is like going into a **strongman's house, you not going to bind him while he gives you his hands and gently allows you to tie him so you can take over his house, no!** He will resist he will fight back he might attack you, **hence deliverance is an act of forceful action to dispossess the strongman.**

> *Every Stubborn Strongman of your fathers house tormenting your life I declare by fire and by force to die now in Jesus name.*

YOUR AUTHORITY VS THE DEVILS AUTHORITY

Let me explain something very important because a lot of Christians are harassed by the devil yet they have authority to harass the devil. In the spirit realm it's all about what you know. Hence the Lord says in Hosea 4:6 that My people perish for lack of knowledge. If you don't know your authority you will pay a heavy price for it. Now let's get to it. The word Power in Greek is in four parts;

- **Dunamis**-which means energy, might, power, great force, it's where we get the word dynamite.
- **Exousia**- delegated authority.
- **Ischuros**- great strength especially physical.
- **Kratos**- Dominion authority.

Now this how it works you have all four of them especially **Exousia** meaning you are in charge, and the devil is not your match or equal because remember in the spirit realm we deal with opposites that are not equal; light and darkness are opposites but they are not equal.

- Life and death are opposites but not equal;
- Sickness and health are opposites but not equal;
- God and the devil are opposites but not equal;
- You and the devil are opposites but not equal.

So the devil can't have all power, but he is an angelic being, he is called the prince of the power of the air. That's why he can kill, steal and destroy. But he cannot touch you because you have Christ in you, who is greater than the one in the world. And remember the devil is defeated Jesus has triumphed over him on the cross. For these reason was the Son of man-made manifest to destroy the works of the devil says 1 John 3:8. This is very important to understand in deliverance ministry. As far as Christ is concerned the devil is defeated he is rendered powerless, but here is the wisdom;

- **So this is what it comes down to; we not fighting for victory but we fighting under victory**, the devil is under our feet, it's only through Christ that we fully subdue him. He has no authority at all actually all Authority is been given unto us according to Luke 10:19; to trample over snakes and scorpions and **over all the power of the enemy** and nothing shall by any means hurt us. Jesus authority given to him in Matthew 28:18 and that **is All Authority from the Father is now ours in Christ. The devil can only use deception and ignorance but as for power he is powerless to us.** Rest assured you are very dangerous and the devil is nothing in the light of the Power of God in you.

So all you need to do is to take your Exousia and Dunamis and kick him out of your life. **The reason why the devil has access into so many lives is because man open doors for him and gives him Exousia (delegated authority) and that means he can do whatever he likes.** Say this pray with me four times out loud:

> *Every authority, power and rights that I have ever given to the devil I take them back now in Jesus Mighty name.*

So we say devil we not begging you, we are not nagging you. We say as Jesus cast out demons by the finger of God, we don't have time to be fighting defeated demons all day and night. **Deliverance has to be by force, with authority; Exousia (delegated authority), rights and with Dunamis power in Jesus Name.**

FASTING AND PRAYER FOR CHAPTER 1

After you have finished with this chapter take a day of fasting and prayer (water only fast) Focus your daily prayer on this DECLARATIONS AND PRAY THEM THOUROUGHLY (spend 5-10 minutes on each point as the Spirit leads you)

MORNING PRAYER

Before you start praying, confess and repent of all sin according to 1John 1:9; *if we confess our sins He is faithful and just to forgive us our sins and to cleanse us from all unrighteousness.*

Confession: Psalm 18:50 *Great deliverance giveth He to His king and showeth mercy to His anointed, to ……………………………… (put your name here), and to my seed* forevermore. (Emphasis added)

MAKE THESE DECLARATIONS OUT LOAD AND PRAY THEM ONE BY ONE

I put on the full amour of God now in Jesus name according to Ephesians 6:10-18
- ➢ The belt of truth
- ➢ The breastplate of righteousness
- ➢ The helmet of salvation
- ➢ The shoes of peace
- ➢ The shield of faith

- the sword of the Spirit
- I position myself in spirit realm and call upon the Lord of Hosts and His Angels of Deliverance to minister on my behalf in Jesus name.
- I soak my spirit soul and body in the blood of Jesus Christ and declare that this is the day of my great deliverance, healing and breakthrough by fire and by force in Jesus name.
- I close every door by the blood of Jesus that was opened by me knowing or unknowingly that might hinder my prayers. I close it now in Jesus name.

AFTERNOON DECLARATIONS

1 **Now touch your head and repeat this several times until you can feel a release**; Jesus Christ of Nazareth Baptize me now with **the Holy Ghost and fire in Jesus Name**.

2 Every strange spirit attacking my life; be destroyed now by fire in Jesus name.

3 Generational bondages, curses and the strongman of my father's house let me loose now by fire in Jesus name.

4 **Touch your naval/stomach as you pray these prayer**; I cut and disconnect myself from any spiritual cord that is connecting me to demonic foundation, altars and human spirits; I cut it now with the sword of the Spirit by fire in Jesus name.

5 I break the spirit of poverty and command every blessing that belongs to me; to be vomited now by the marine serpent in Jesus name.

6 I disconnect myself from marine altars and demonic dreams; I disconnect my life from their influence in Jesus name.

7 I destroy the spiritual wife/ spiritual husband assigned to destroy my life; I arrest them now by fire in Jesus name.

8 I renounce every involvement in the demonic kingdom that I have ever entered into.

9 I destroy every contract binding my destiny in Jesus name.

10   I call down fire upon every assembly of the kingdom of darkness assigned to destroy me. Let fire consume them now in Jesus name.
11   I receive total deliverance from demonic covenants.
12   I shall live and not die to proclaim the glory of God.

13   Every Evil monitoring spirit, monitoring my progress; be arrested now by fire in Jesus name.
14   Enemies of progress against my success be paralyzed by fire and die in Jesus name
15   I take all my riches, gifts and blessing held up by the serpent in Jesus name
16   I take my prayer life back now in Jesus name.
17   Holy Ghost fire, purge my life completely in Jesus name.
18   I claim my complete deliverance in the name of Jesus Christ from all domestic demonic covenants in Jesus Mighty name.
19   **Lay your hand on your head and another on your stomach or naval and begin to pray like this**; Holy Ghost fire, burn from the top of my head to the sole of my feet now in Jesus name.
20   I accelerate from bondage to freedom in every area of my life in Jesus name.
21   I command every evil plantation in my life; Come out now by fire with all your roots in Jesus might name.
22   Every evil stranger in my body I cast you out now by fire in Jesus mighty name (**Begin to touch you head, neck, chest, stomach etc. And keep repeating this prayer**).
23   I take my authority and legal rights in Jesus mighty name.

CHAPTER 2

THE HOLY GHOST FIRE AND HIS BAPTISM

Are you ready to move to a higher life? A life of the Spirit and fire, I am happy to announce to you that; It is it your right and inheritance. A promise delayed is not a promise denied. In this chapter I stand in agreement with you for a mighty visitation of the Spirit of God and fire that will alter your life and give you a testimony that will bless you for the rest of your life.

Always remember this, **before God can use you or give you anything He must first make you (prepare you); this is the secret to Gods riches and Power**. Start praying; 'Lord make me' first, then once you are made; then the gifts and the blessings will come. That is where the Holy Ghost Fire comes in. It's in the fire that we are made pure vessels ready for the Masters service. The fire molds our character, makes us candidates for Gods hand and blessings. **God is more interested in your character, that in your gifts and blessings. Your charisma, your gifts or intellect can open doors for you, but it is your character that will keep them open.** How many gifted people out there are living wasted lives because they failed to maintain good positions or opportunities due to their character? **Your character is so important it will decide whether you go to heaven or not.**

It is the fire that ultimately prepares us, sanctifies us so that when the trumpet sounds one day we are ready to meet with the Lord as a pure Church, holy and acceptable unto Him. But that's not all the fire is there for. I discuss in this chapter at least four areas that the Fire is meant to address in our lives and its purpose. Before we get to that let me touch on a few things that will prepare you for the fire.

GODS CALENDER

Where are you in Gods timing? There is a spiritual calendar in the spiritual realm concerning your life, some people are still trapped in the Old Testament, they observe all the laws of Moses and spend all their lives living by the law, others are in their set timing; they are living in Gods time for their lives . In the 21st century we are living in the era of grace, the era of the Holy Ghost and fire. There was an era of the Father or the era of the Laws of God in the Old Testament, then Jesus came in the New Testament or dispensation to bring salvation and fulfillment of the law, but in these last days we are in the era of the Holy Ghost and Fire. After Jesus comes to take His Church the Spirit of God will leave this earth. We have a window of grace to live in the greatest time in all eternity past, present and future. This is a very powerful season and you and I have been called to live in it. 1 peter 1:10-12 puts it like this;

Of this salvation the prophets have inquired and searched carefully who prophesied of the grace that would come to you, searching what, or what manner of time the Spirit of Christ who was in them was indicating when He testified before hand the sufferings of Christ and the glories that will follow. To them it was revealed that not to themselves, but to us they were ministering the things which now have been reported to you through those who have preached the gospel to you by the Holy Spirit sent from heaven- things which angels desire to look into.

You are loaded with the greatest blessing of all times you are here to display the glory of God in its fullness there will never be such a time. This is the season where God is calling His people to a higher life, a life of the Spirit, a life of power, righteousness and grace. It's yours for the taking. Declare this prayer out load;
- ➢ O Lord; arise and shine through me, for my light has come and Your glory is risen within me.
- ➢ Let your Fire fall upon me now and use me for Your glory.
- ➢ My father if I am presently wrongly scheduled, Reschedule Me according to your calendar in Jesus name.

PROPHETIC WORD "MESSENGERS OF FIRE"

(A Prophetic Word during the writing of this chapter)
As I was writing this book the Lord began to whisper these Words to me;
'**Messengers of Fire!**' *My messengers of Fire! Speak to My messengers of Fire.*

Then the Lord said; the season and time has come for His fire to be released on the earth. He says this is not the fire of judgment but His Holy fire that He is releasing to all who will believe in His name. He is raising the no name brands, the unknowns the ones that no one knows about, they are going to turn this world upside down with My fire says the Lord. I have them hidden in small insignificant places but they will begin to feel my fire in their bones, in their bellies and in their hearts. They will forsake everything for my sake, they will refuse to fit in. they will be so consumed in my will that the world will cease to exist for them, they will have enough to share and be a blessing. They are all over, some in the market places some in the churches some in their hidden places. This era is for them, they are called Messengers of Fire.

They will render witches jobless, demons will scattered at their command, they will set homes and cities on fire, the sick will be healed through them the lost will be found, the bound delivered, I am releasing an anointing that will empty hospitals, not 10% or 50% will be touched anymore but 100% ,everyone will be touched. All who sit under their ministry will experience God. I will enable them do to miracles that have never been seen they will recreate things that have never been done. I have put my mark on them and whoever touches them or contents with them will have to face me. I will be their God and they will be My people.

Enough is enough the satanic kingdom will tremble at their presence they will loose many Satanist and devil worshippers they will bring my end time harvest and be mightily used of God. I have chosen them, I have anointed them. My Fire is upon them and I am the Lord, who does these things, and you say when Lord? And I the Lord have spoken swiftly; quickly all of this will come to pass. In a moment you will see them manifest. This very time in your lifetime you will meet them. Says the Lord of Host.

Many have anticipated the end time revival that will start from Cape to Cairo and impact the whole world. Many have prayed about it, My people have repented and I have seen their hearts, I have heard their sorrow, and now I come to deliver them. I am ready to pour out my blessing on the land, every one of my children is special and I want the world to see who I am through them. Many have suffered and been tested to the utter most, but the seasons are changing, wipe your tears for you are one of them, My messenger of fire. Yes that is what they will be called messengers of Fire.

Your season of joy has come, after you have been tested you have come through, you are an overcome, use your testimony to lift up others. I am going to release My power ,ministering angels will be seen everywhere in this season, the fullness of the gifts of the Holy Ghost will be common and the supernatural will be so familiar that everyone will see it. I am the Lord who has spoken.
May it be done to you according to His Word in Jesus name I Pray Amen.

WE NEED THE FIRE

The Holy Ghost and Fire Baptism is a very precious gift from God. Many of us are baptized with the Holy Spirit, speak in tongues, and it ends there. Unless you experience the Holy Ghost and Fire baptism, you may take a very long time to reach the fullness of the power & glory of God. We need to be baptized with the fullness of the Holy Ghost and Fire as to allow God to refine and purify us (Matthew 3:11, Luke 3:16). My prayer to you is that; you will begin to hunger and thirst for the fullness of this gift, don't settle for the shaking and falling under the power, no! Go further, go deeper and seek the Spirit of God and the Fire that comes with Him. Because you cannot separate the two. We have devil worshippers seating in our services and destroying Gods people, because the church is lacking fire. It's time for the fire of God to come upon His Church. And it's going to start with you.

HOW IS THE SPIRIT LIKE FIRE AND WHAT IS HIS PURPOSE?

The Bible is filled with scriptures that illustrate that God is Fire. Remember when we speak about God we cannot exclude the Holy Spirit who happens to be the Power of God. Fire is a sign of Gods power in 1 kings 18:38 the Bible declares that the fire of the Lord fell and consumed the burned sacrifices and the wood and the stones and the dust and it licked up the water that was in the trench. The sight was so amazing that all faces fell down and said that the Lord God, He is God.

In verse 24 of the same chapter Elijah made this statement; he said, call on the names of your gods and I will call on the name of the Lord; **and the God who answers by fire He is God.** May He answer you by Fire in Jesus name. You see, God is ready to respond to your prayers, He is waiting on the Elijah's of today to take their stand against the false prophets and kingdom of darkness. The fire of God is ready to fall down and demonstrate Gods power upon the wicked. It was His fire that brought glory to Him. May His fire be demonstrated in your life against those who fight you and may they be put to shame in Jesus name.

FIRE IS A WONDERFUL PICTURE OF THE WORK OF THE HOLY SPIRIT. THE SPIRIT IS LIKE FIRE AT LEAST IN FOUR DIFFERENT WAYS;
1. **HE IS GODS PRESENCE**
2. **HE IS USED IN DELIVERANCE**
3. **HE BRINGS GODS PASSION**
4. **HE WORKS GODS PURITY OR SANCTIFICATION**

Let's start with **GODS PRESENCE**;
In the Old Testament, God showed His presence to the Israelites by overspreading the tabernacle with fire in Numbers 9: 15 the Word says; now on the day that the tabernacle was raised up, the cloud covered the tabernacle, the tent of the testimony from evening until morning it was above the tabernacle **like the appearance of fire**.
Verse 18 says: As long as the cloud stayed above the tabernacle they remained encamped.
The cloud represented the presence of the Lord, the tent represents you and me, the Spirit of the Lord as a cloud like fire is resting upon you and me. The Old Testament is a very interesting, we learn so much about our God. Did you know that every child of God should have this cloud upon them? I will never forget the encounter I heard long before I knew this scripture; I remember feeling a shade of his presence upon my head. It literally felt like a shade or covering of heat, sometimes it was like a mist. These things are spiritual and we that are living in the New Testament should live in them every day. His Presence is not only upon us, but within us. We Are led by Him as He leads we follow. Moses said of His presence; Lord let me not go from here without your Presence I would rather stay, for what will distinguish us

from the rest of the world. It's His presence. Whenever you walk into a place amongst the lost His presence should be felt. I have heard people come up to me and say; you are pastor right? They didn't know me but they sense the difference. What separates us from the world is His Presence.

David had such a revelation of His presence that he prayed Oh that I may dwell in the house of the Lord all the days of my life to inquire in His temple. The Presence of God means His face and His eyes. We are safe when He is with us. Call upon His presence today. Create a dwelling for Him. He dwells in the mists of His praise. Cultivate a life of His presence. Always seek to acknowledge Him in everything. Greet him in the morning, ask Him what to wear, what to do, talk with Him. Make it your daily routine to just chat with Him. Journal what He says and be His vessel.

Pray from your heart this prayer and sense the breath of His presence and His fire;

- Cloud of the Lord rest upon my life now in Jesus name.
- Let me know you are here with me, let me feel your presence my Lord.
- Fire of His Presence lead me now I pray in Jesus name.
- Lord baptize me now with your Holy Ghost and fire of your Presence in Jesus name.
- Lord make me too hot for the devil to handle me in Jesus Name.

Secondly Fire is used in **GODS DELIVERANCE**:

God said to His people Israel when He was bringing them to the land they will go and possess and cast away nations before them, the Bible calls them great and mighty nations. God said in verse 2 of Deuteronomy 7; that when the Lord God **delivers** them (the nations before them) over to Israel, Israel shall conquer them and utterly destroy them. Israel shall make no covenant with them or show mercy to them. But this is what Israel shall do to them verse 5; **But thus shall you deal with them; you shall destroy their altars, break their sacred pillars, cut down their wooden images, and burn their curved images with fire.**

God gives His people a mighty deliverance by instructing them to deal with their enemies. They are to break down some things, cut on others, but with curved images they must burn them with fire. Curved images speak of Idols or the likenesses of God; for most of African people this are ancestral demonic contact points that are depicted in form of carved images. **These images are contact points with the demonic spirits and the devil uses them to bind so many people.** People like to see in order to believe, they will rather worship a piece of wood because they can see it rather that worshipping God. This practice is a curse and if you come from a family where ancestors or Idols were worshipped I urge you to address those areas and pray for total deliverance by fire in Jesus Name. **Anything that was made to be worshipped was to be burned with fire. This is picture of deliverance.** Whenever God wants to set his people free He will always address such areas as altars, foundations, ancestors and Idols. They are strongholds and generational covenants that might be holding down people. God wants you separated from them. Holy Ghost fire is an agent of great deliverance.

The devil can hold people and generations bound through these demonic altars but Gods fire is there for us to use to destroy those forces.

Call down the Fire of God now upon any generational demonic altars, pillars demonic foundations, family Idols and strongholds that are limiting you from experiencing Gods fullness;

Declare these powerful prayers now;

- ➢ I consume every shrine of demonic family altars speaking against my destiny by fire now in Jesus name.
- ➢ Let stones of fire pursue and dominate all the strongholds in my life in Jesus name.
- ➢ I smash the head of my family Idol, Idols of ancestors I destroy you now by fire in Jesus name.
- ➢ I dismantle demonic altars from my fathers and mothers side in Jesus name.
- ➢ Every demonic strongman and associated spirits of financial collapse, receive the hail stones of fire now in Jesus name.
- ➢ Every ancestral connection in my life I disconnect myself from you now by fire in Jesus name.
- ➢ Every ancestral dream pollution, I release myself from you in Jesus name

- Every demonic names that come from my family altars I renounce them in Jesus name

In Deuteronomy 9:1-3 the Word of the Lord declares;

Hear, O Israel: You are to cross over the Jordan and go in to dispossess nations great and mighty than yourself, cities great and fortified up to heaven, a people great and tall, the descendants of Anakim, whom you know, and of whom you heard it said; Who can stand before the descendants of Anak ?
Therefore understand therefore this day that the Lord thy God is he which goes before you; **as a consuming fire** *He shall destroy them and shall bring them down before your face; so shalt you drive them out and destroy them quickly, as the Lord has said unto thee.*

Anyone or anything be it a stronghold, a power, a force or a spirit in the way of you and your promise, set you mind to it now and **then based on what you just read, look in four directions and repeat this prayer 21 times for each direction until you feel a breakthrough:** *Pick the appropriate one. (Mountain of debts, spirit of demotion, lack, sickness, household enemies etc.)*
- **Holy Ghost Fire! X 21 times**

I celebrate with you and praise God with you, **the grip of the devil has been loosed, maintain your ground and keep believing, you will begin to notice a change in your dreams and those enemies that had demonic plans concerning you, they are going to see God elevate you, expect a major breakthrough to come in next 7 days from now**. Stay humble and faithful to God in every way. Jesus Christ loves you and has predestined your freedom in Jesus name let it be so.

Thirdly the Fire brings **GODS PASSION;**
After the two travelling disciples talked with the resurrected Jesus they described their hearts as burning within them (Luke 24:32). After the Apostles received the baptism of the Holy Ghost and fire they had such a passion that the world had never seen, they proclaimed and demonstrated the Word of God boldly. The number one recipe for success in any field is

passion. We are called to be passionate lovers of God. **Loves of God will always outrun workers of God.** It is that burning passion that drives us to do the things that we do. Jesus was passionate about His ministry, He spend all His life doing what He loved.

Are you serving God out of duty or passion? Do you give because you have to or because you love God? Do you serve God out of your own strength? **I see passion as an anointing; a divine ability to carry out Gods task.** Without it we can't change the world. May the Spirit of burning, Spirit of passion ignite your life with passion for His kingdom. That you will be so consumed in the things of God that nothing else matters. Put your priorities in order. God is your first love. Have you ever wondered why the first and greatest commandment is to love God? I believe God wants us to focus our lives on Him, make Him the only one that matters, because that's what we were created for; it was for Him and His Pleasure. **There is no greater satisfaction in live without loving God above everything.** Allow His Sprit to give you love for him. Fall in love with him, write and sing Him love songs, and give him you heart and affection. That's the best thing you can ever do for yourself. And the Fire of God is availing all that to you. Pray softly from your heart;

> ➢ Fire of God; ignite my spirit, soul and body to love God more than anything in this world.
> ➢ Fire of God; give me a burning passion to fix my eyes on Jesus, and not on man.
> ➢ Fire of God; envelope my life with the passion for the things of God.

Fourthly He brings **GODS PURITY AND SANCTIFICATION;**
God wants you pure and zealous for good works (Titus 2:14). But He needs to put us through fire and refine us. The Psalmist puts it like this **For you; O God have tested us; you have refined us as silver is refined** Psalm 66:10. The best agent to refine silver is with fire. Are you the elect of God then you need the fire; 1 peter 1:2 adds and says to you and me;
*Elect according to the foreknowledge of God the Father in **sanctification of the Spirit for obedience** and sprinkling of the blood of Jesus Christ.*

The refining fire of the Holy Ghost is there to prepare us for service. It is only after going through the refining & purifying process of Fire, that God can fully use us in the fullness of His power & glory. There are things that God must deal with in our lives and He uses His purifying fire to burn them away; sometimes it's not an easy process; but if you will allow Him to put you through the fire you will come out pure as gold, fit for the Masters use. God wants to deal with areas such as;

- Selfishness; God wants self out of the way so He can be seen through you.
- Our wrong motives that are against God's will for our life.
- The dross of wrong intentions and evil sinful desires.
- Resistance that the enemy puts in our minds that prevents us from proclaiming God's message.
- Doubt and unbelief.
- Pride.
- Fear of man; what others think of you.
- Lack of zeal and love for God things.

David Herzog wrote, **"If you try to cast away darkness but you yourself are not full of light, chances are you will take a long time to do it.** When you are full of the glory of God, often one word from God will expel all the darkness away."

Read this Scripture and pray earnestly for the Refining fire to deal with every area of your life that is not surrendered to God fully:

- **Zechariah 13:9, "This third I will bring into the fire; I will refine them as silver and test them like gold. They will call on my name and I will answer them; I will say, they are my people, and they will say, 'The Lord is our God.'"**

- O Lord according to you word refine me as silver and test me as gold.
- Let all evil motives, selfishness and unbelief be burned by your fire in Jesus Name.
- Remove a heart of stone and give me a heart of flesh.

- ➤ Lord do not let me escape your refining process, purify me, cleans me, make me whole.
- ➤ Let my first love come back, my zeal, my fire, my unshakable faith in you and my boldness in Jesus name.
- ➤ Forgive me Lord for standing in the way of Your fire and Your will for my life
- ➤ I surrender all to You in Jesus name.

We need to be prepared, we need to be made ready, the task ahead is huge and time is running out. May the Lords fire purge us and may He find pleasure in using us. In Jesus name.

THE FIRE AND ANOINTING

When the Holy Ghost fire of God falls upon you, so too does the anointing of God. I like to call it; **the anointing fire or the FIRE ANOINTING this is the one God uses to commission His people into the work He has for them.**

*But you shall **receive power when the Holy Ghost has come upon you** and you shall be **witness for Me** in Judea, in Samaria, and to the ends of the earth. Acts 1:8*
*In Hebrews 1:7 He says; Who makes His Angels, spirits And His **ministers, flame of fire.***

I am using these two references of scripture to say that God anoints, Holy fire comes even as it came on the day of Pentecost with the Spirit of God. You are called to be a living, talking fire; it's your duty to go out there and display Gods power. May you beginning to feel the anointing of the Holy Spirit upon your life, the tangible felt anointing that will enable you to do things that you cannot do in your own strength. **The Fire anointing is the empowering presence of God that enables us to do God given assignments by demonstrating Gods power over the kingdom of darkness.**

Declare these prayers out loud;

- ➤ **O Lord according to Hebrews 1:7 and Acts 1:8 above baptize me with the Holy Ghost and fire, make me a flame to witness to the lost, ignite my spiritual life with a passion for souls. Lord anoint me now with you fire anointing so that I can** spread you glory to the world. Appoint me as your messenger of fire and let the bound be set free through my life and testimony in Jesus name.

(This prayer above God spoke to me that whoever will pray it earnestly will experience this fire anointing, most of you will start bubbling from your spirit, and you will feel like talking in tongues. Some will even experience laughing in the spirit don't stop keep flowing in the anointing and God will do the rest.)

Now let's use the Fire to pray;

- O Lord let the Lightning of the Flashing Spear according to Habakkuk 3:11; Flash and thunder upon every antichrist spirit assigned to delay my progress in Jesus mighty name.
- According to Habakkuk 3:4, O Lord ignite my hands and let the rays flash from my hands where power is hidden in Jesus name.
- Make my eyes like that of Jesus; eyes like a blazing fire according to Revelation 1:14; let wickedness tremble at my sight in Jesus name.
- Let there be thunder according to Psalm 29:3 against my enemies in Jesus name.
- I call forth the lightning of heaven according to 2 Samuel 22:15, Job 36:22 upon every assembly of darkness assigned over my life, my family and my church.

Are you desperate for Gods anointing upon your life; do you want this fire? Start seeking God today, **He is putting that desire in you because He wants to use you, respond.** Pay the price and carry your cross. Put God first above everything. As the Lord says, "Call to me and I will answer you and tell you great and mighty things, which you do not know" (Jeremiah 33:3).

- There is a special fast at the end of this chapter for three days; prepare yourself God is about to elevate you. I have included with the fast an impartation prayer for the Fire Anointing to come upon you. Please try and set time aside daily in the mornings or evening to pray through these prayers.

FELLOWSHIP WITH THE HOLY SPIRIT

Yes! This is your season and time to experience Him like never before, He is been longing to reveal Himself to you. He loves to fellowship with you more than anything else. He wants you spirit soul and body, he wants to wear you like a glove and use you powerfully for Gods glory. Jesus said of Him it is for your advantage that I go for unless I do not go, the Spirit will not come. He was in creation as the Power of God to create the universe. He always was and always will be. He is the one who inspired man and woman of the Bible to do exploits for God. Without Him we cannot make it in this walk of faith. He opens our spiritual eyes to see. The world does not know Him. He is the one and only Spirit of the Living God. He is the Called the HOLY SPIRIT.

WE DON'T USE HIM, BUT HE USES US, WE DO NOT POSSESS THE HOLY GHOST, NO! HE POSSESSES US.

He is God co-eternal, co-equal and co-existing with the Father and the Son. His Name is called the Holy Spirit, the third person of the trinity. **He is not some force or power you can use however you want, no! He is the Living God and must be given honor glory and dominion that He deserves.** It is very important that we are taught right about the Holy Spirit because He is everything to us now on earth. The Lord is serious about this matter. We need to be put in order, the Spirit owns the church. We are called to co-labor with Him in submission.

IF YOU WANT TO KNOW HIM IN POWER, YOU FIRST NEED TO KNOW HIM IN PERSON.

I like it when the Bible says the grace of our Lord Jesus Christ, the love of God and **the fellowship of the Holy Spirit be with us now and forevermore**. It's all about fellowship with the Holy Spirit; there are three levels of prayer or fellowship with God;
- There is Praying to God
- Praying with God
- And Praying from God

I won't go into details on them now, but I want you to see these that your prayer live will consists of the three following levels. The first one being the beginners level. We all pray to God and its very Biblical, but there is a higher dimension, **where we pray with God it's the realm of fellowship with Him we are not looking up to him, but we are sitting and dining with him.** We talk or pray and listen and He talks back. This is fellowship with the Holy Spirit, He is our companion, and He wants to speak to us, commune with us. He is the *Parakletos* the one who is beside us. So let's not stop at praying to God but let's pray with Him, listen to His heart and do what He wants, not what we want. The Holy Spirit is present in the earth today to manifest the sons of the kingdom. He will not let you down; and He will be involved in every area of your life.

PROPHETIC WORD "SUPERNATURAL LIVING"
(Prophetic Word during my fellowship time with the Holy Spirit)

God began to speak to me strongly about the supernatural living, He spoke in such a way that I had to include this word, especially for those who hunger and love to see the God of the Bible in today's world.

'My son the season and time has come for supernatural living, my children have been so consumed by the spirit of the world and the natural order that, they cease to see beyond their problems. Many pray but don't see answers because they limit me. They live in the world of limitation and I the Lord cannot be limited by man. They live in a realm I didn't die for them to live in, the realm of space, time and matter. I am calling my sons and daughters to go past the natural into the supernatural, the realm of eternity, the realm of power the realm of faith, where there are no limits, no boundaries. My children must stop praying and believing for small things, I am your limitless God, who does the supernatural. I want them to taste the blessings of the Lord. Man has taught that it's only the human intellect that makes one superior and people think that they are to live and survive by intellectualism and knowledge. But I the Lord am saying you were designed to live supernaturally, through the power of God, here on the natural earth. I want you to taste heaven now, and not when you die. Live from above; live with no limits, live as though you are supernatural because that's who you are. No limits, no more. Those who

will pursue these life, I will reward them says the Lord. I am tired of dead works, fleshly natural efforts they don't please me, says the Lord, because I don't want you to use your power, but my power. I am brining this revelation upon my children. This is the answer to victorious living, this is what the scripture refers to when it says; ' the wind blows where it wishes no one knows where it comes from, no one knows where it's going, so is everyone who is born of the Spirit'.

MY HOLY GHOST AND FIRE BAPTISM

Several years ago I took a fast of 21 days; it had been six months since my conversion and baptism in water. But I had not been baptized in the Holy Spirit and fire. It was a very strange period of my life because I could not accept the fact that the promise is there in the Bible and it's almost six months and I am not baptized in the Holy Spirit so I was very uncomfortable. I remember going to so many churches to seek this gift of baptism. I went to one church where I was rolled on the floor several times, I went to one church where they said fake the tongues until you get it right, I went to another where they said I have to wait at least a year. But my confidence was on this words my pastor used to say: **a promise delayed is not a promise denied.**

So I waited and on the eve of my last day of the fast I broke the fast and thanked the Lord for the baptism in faith. I felt it's done and I will keep waiting earnestly for the manifestation. So the next morning after all this prayers and fasting and experiences my leaders asked if we could do one more prayer as we had spent the whole night together in one place. So before we departed we assembled to pray and while they stretched their hands towards me without touching me; a strong wind came upon me and it threw me to the ground and there it was; a river broke out of my belly, I literally felt like a rushing stream flowing out. I remembered the words of Jesus; ***for out of your belly will flow rivers of living water***. It was happening I was receiving the baptism of the Holy Ghost and fire it was so amazing, I was speaking in unknown tongues and crying for over 45 minutes. There was a background song playing repeatedly saying;

> Lord sends the rain, pour out your Sprit, Let the fire fall, heal us all in all, pour it afresh on me. (Same verse over and over)

The song was on repeat and it went on and I went on and on and there I was filled with the Holy Ghost and fire. Since then I prayed for everything in tongues, my food, my traveling, and my life was just filled with tongues. I spoke several other tongues witnessed and saw the power of God in my life. This was an experience that changed my life. **I believe every born again child of God should have this encounter because it is a promise to all of us**. There is no way you can expect to have victory in this life without the baptism of the Holy Ghost and fire.

THE HOLY GHOST BAPTSIM IS SEPARATE FROM THE SALVATION EXPERIENCE.
> **Was I not filled with the spirit when I accepted Jesus Christ?**

There is a lot of confusion and ignorance on this question Jesus is called the Savior and the baptizer with the Holy Ghost and fire. Be aware that those are two different names and functions. So yes you did receive the Holy Spirit when you accepted Jesus Christ but that doesn't end there, there is a second experience called the baptism of the Holy Spirit and fire. If you haven't received this baptism pray these prayers softly with all your heart, repeat them several times until you can feel a difference put this book aside and for 5-10 minutes pray earnestly;
> Jesus Christ baptism me now with the Holy Spirit and fire.
> I stand on your promised word that cannot lie, I await you Spirit
> Holy Spirit and fire; fall upon me know in Jesus Name.

In **Acts 19:2** Paul comes to Ephesus and poses this question to the believers; **"Have you received the Holy Ghost since you believed?"**
In other words baptism is not when we converted to Christ. **Conversion is repenting away from sin toward God. Whereas baptism in the Holy Ghost and fire is something that Christ does for us; it is a gift from God.** The Bible says in Luke 11:13 that The Father will give the Holy Spirit to them that ask Him. It is a gift and you don't even have to fast or struggle to receive

these gift. The simplest way to receive from God is by faith. I have heard people who were baptized in their sleep, in their work place some while they sat in their living rooms, others in times of worship. Ask, seek and knock until you receive don't settle for average. Remember I spoke about taking your things by force. Learn to P.U.S.H; Pray Until Something Happens.

BAPTISM IS A SYMBOL OF PURIFICATION AND CONSECRATION. THERE ARE TWO BAPTISMS;

1. **The Water baptism** with immersion is when a person is immersed in water. But in water baptism the water is not in you. It's simply a place where you bury the old nature and when you come out of the water the Bible says you are now a new creature. You are now raised to life and you should reckon ourselves dead to sin but alive to God in Christ our Lord (Romans 6:11)

2. **Baptism with the Holy Ghost and Fire** is a spiritual immersion unto the life of God, the Supernatural life of God. The life of His Spirit in us. It is the baptism into the power of God. It puts you are under the influence of the Spirit of God, you walk in the Spirit of God, and you are filled with the Spirit of God, for the Holy Ghost is in you. (1 Corinthians 6:19). The fire of God is you, the lamp of His Spirit is in you, and you are a living, talking, walking fire of God. You are in Him and He in you. I like how Hebrews 1:7 puts it; In speaking of the Angels He says He makes His angels, spirits and His servants, flame of fire. You are His flame of fire in the earth; you are His agent on a mission to destroy the works of darkness. Fire is your middle name. Wherever you go His fire is with you to impact lives and bring deliverance. Be enveloped in His Fire. Pray this prayer with your hands lifted up;

> ➢ **Lord envelope me with your Holy Ghost and fire in Jesus Name.**

EXPERIENCING THE FIRE IN THE BAPTISM

So after my Holy Ghost and Fire baptism the river flowed and I was never the same since, I literally felt possessed by the Spirit of God. In within the baptism was the presence of the Lord so strong and tangible. It felt like fire in my bones and in my hands. It was like a Jeremiah experience of fire in his bones. I had such supernatural experience in the natural. When the Baptism of fire comes you become heaven bound and you live in the supernatural. So the fire felt as it was in Acts 2:3, I felt it on my body and on my head. At times it will feel like an oil flowing down my face. At times I felt it in my belly on my hands. There are many ways you can sense the presence of fire. But here is one thing you'll notice the fire of God will keep you hungry and on fire for the Lord. It's a passion that you feel inside of you. **And the key to maintaining this supernatural living is praying in tongues.**

PRAYING IN TONGUES IS THE DOORWAY TO SPIRITUAL GIFTS AND SUPERNATUAL LIVING

This is probably the most important lesson to many believers out there who have received the gift of tongues. I know God wants you to know this so you can progress deeper into the fullness of the gifts of the Holy Spirit such as prophecy, Words of Knowledge, Working of miracles, just to mention a few. Now why tongues? Jesus Christ on the day of Pentecost opened the heavens and the baptism of the Spirit of God fell upon the 120 in the upper room. They spoke in other tongues as the Spirit gave them utterance. We are told that this was a supernatural experience and the people who heard them were confused (Acts 1 and 2). Since then the Church broke into the Spirit realm and power was at their disposal. **Signs and wonders followed and WHENEVER they prayed they used this new language.** Let's see why I am saying this;

In acts 6: 4 the twelve apostles made a commitment that I want you to understand its full meaning. They said; *but we will give ourselves continually* **to prayer** *and to the ministry of the word* (according to NKJV). Now here is the knowledge;

The original Greek text reads like this (Acts 6:4); *we moreover in* **the prayer** *and the ministry of the word.* Note **the prayer** as opposed to; *to prayer.* Now what's the difference?

The prayer is obviously different from any prayer. **The prayer is specific and this prayer *(the prayer)* the Bible was referring to was the prayer of tongues.**

This was a major shift as you can imagine the church had never known anything of this nature, so *the prayer* **of tongues was the ultimate prayer.** It represented the power of the Spirit and fire; it represented Pentecost and the fulfillment of the promise from the Lord Jesus Christ. So this is what you and I need to do. The church has minimized praying in tongues, very seldom do believers gather to pray *the prayer*. But God is revealing this to you so that you can start praying *the prayer*. This is the gateway to the all the nine gifts of the Holy Spirit. You give yourself to *the prayer* and the rest will follow.

The Bible says we are to pray without ceasing; now how on earth can you and I manage this? The answer is we can't. It's only praying in the Spirit or in tongues that we can pray continually. This prayer edifies you, builds your spirit man it stirs the gifts of God. I believe the secret is out there now. A man by the name of Smith Wigglesworth discovered this secret and prayed every day an hour in tongues. And he became one of Gods generals in our history books. It's time to pray **the Prayer**.

> ➤ Take a few minutes and pray in the Spirit now, and every time you get the opportunity pray in the Spirit. Your life will never be the same again in Jesus Name. May grace be grated you to be diligent and committed in this.

FASTING AND PRAYER CHAPTER 2

Congratulations on completing this second Chapter, You will take 3 days fasting now. I advise you to keep reading but go through the prayers below thoroughly and I know your life will never be the same after this. (This fasting is a water only fast from day 1 to day 3; take the fast in the days that is suitable for you)

THREE DAYS BAPTISM OF FIRE

The best and most powerful way to crush the oppressor is to be baptized with the fire of the Holy Ghost. Where there is no fire there will always be oppression. Have you notice some areas in your life where the enemy attacks and manipulates your life? This is an indication that you need the fire of God.

Remember the key is to receive in faith, it's your right as a born again child of God. These prayers are to restore and revive your lost fire and glory, do them with all your heart and your life will never be the same again. Even if you are already baptized in the Holy Ghost take this opportunity to rekindle the fire.

DAY 1 SCRIPTURES AND PRAYERS (Spend 2-5 minutes on each Prayer point)

Spend time in Praise and Worship read John 14: 15-18 'Jesus Promises another Helper.'

Read Acts 1:8, Acts 2: 1-39
NB. IF YOU HAVE BEEN ALREADY BAPTISED IN THE HOLY GHOST AND FIRE AND YOU SPEAK IN OTHER TONGUES. SPEND 30 MIN TO AND HOUR PRAYING IN TONGUES DAILY THROUGHOUT THIS FASTING. THERE IS ALWAYS MORE YOU CAN RECEIVE FROM GOD

1. Thank God for your life.
2. Thank God for the power of His Holy Spirit.
3. Confess all your sins and repent.
4. Call upon the Father to fill you with His Holy Spirit and fire (this is your focus for the next 3 days, Pray this prayer in your heart all day with expectation)
5. Father in the name of Jesus incubate me with your fire now I pray.
6. Every anti-power bondage upon my life, I command it to break now in Jesus name.
7. O lord ignite my spiritual life with fire, ignite my soul with fire, ignite my body with fire.

DAY 2 PRAYERS AND PROPHETIC ACTIONS (Spend 2-5minutes on each Prayer point)

Read 1kings 18:20- 40 'Elijah Mount Carmel Victory', and Jeremiah 20:9
The fire of God is the key to rescue the bound from the shekels of demons.
Today you are going to cancel all false fires and anti-Christ negative

anointing ever spoken upon your life. Every false hand or impartation ever done on you it's going to depart today as you allow the fresh fire of God to deliver you.

1. Thank God for the purifying Power of fire of the Holy Ghost in your life.
2. Cover yourself and your family with the blood of Jesus.
3. Anoint your House with anointing oil (olive oil preferably that has been prayed for) and consecrate your prayer life your prayer altar unto God. (You may ask your Pastor for guidance and prayer for this part.)
4. O lord let your fire that destroys all pollution from the kingdom of Satan fall upon me now in Jesus name.
5. I release myself from any negative anointing's in Jesus name.
6. I release myself from marine spirits and false anointing's in Jesus name.
7. Every door that I have opened knowingly or unknowingly of spiritual leakage be shut by fire now in Jesus name.
8. I command the fire of God upon every organ in my body (touch from your head, ears, you mouth, your chest your stomach, mention your inner organs all the way to your feet) Holy Ghost fire touch me now in Jesus name.
9. Every hindrance is broken; I command an open heaven now in Jesus name.

DAY 3 DECLARATIONS

Today you say good bye to lukewarm, powerless life. God wants you either hot or cold. You are taking a step into joining the generals in the faith. You are taking a step into a life of a massager of fire. This is serious business and I urge you to maintain this lifestyle and prayers. God's grace is sufficient, be blessed as you seal your baptism today and take up your position in the spiritual combat. Remember you are protected and need not fear those with you are more that those with them.
Read 2Kings 6: 8-18

Receive these prophetic declarations from me by faith in Jesus name;
- I degree and declare that your eyes will be opened to see in the Spiritual realm in Jesus name.
- I degree and declare you will see the messengers of heaven the angelic host ministering on your behalf.
- I degree and declare you will move in the supernatural power of God.
- I degree and declare you are free indeed, from any form of demonic attack or curse.
- I degree your provision has come in Jesus name.
- I degree your financial freedom has come in Jesus name.
- I degree your promotion is come.
- I degree you deliverance is due.
- I degree your healing is due.
- I degree your inheritance is due.
- I degree divine protection is your portion.
- I degree permanent Breakthrough and Blessings upon your Life.
- I degree the sun, moon and stars to favor you, by day and by night.
- I degree divine immunity from demonic attacks upon your life
- In Jesus name, receive it now I pray Amen.

RECEIVE THE IMPARTATION OF THE HOLY GHOST AND FIRE (Pray this prayer out load and continue to receive)

'Father in the mighty Name of Jesus Christ I stand on your promises. You said that you will pour out your Spirit in this last days upon all flesh, you said that you will baptize me with your Holy Spirit and with fire, you promised that upon mount Zion there shall be deliverance and holiness and the house of Jacob shall possess her possessions and house of Joseph a flame. I believe this promise is for me and I ask now for an impartation of your Spirit of fire, I believe that this is the anointing for this season and you are raising messengers of fire. I believe that I am one of them. I receive now this gift and expect to experience You in a new and revived

way. Thank you Holy Spirit, use me know to spread this fire wherever I go, that the name of Jesus will be glorified and the name of Satan put to shame. In Jesus name I pray. Amen.'

Today spend the day singing songs of Praise and Worship you have received now go and spread the fire of God. **Freely you have received freely give. Remember the key to receive more from God is to keep giving away. End off and seal everything with these prayers;**

1. Every power of darkness following me around be destroyed by fire in Jesus name.
2. I degree the arrows of my enemies upon me to backfire in Jesus name.
3. Holy Ghost arise in me and promote me.
4. Vehicle of my destiny be repaired and put back on the road of my success in Jesus name.
5. O Lord sent me divine help and associations in Jesus name.
6. O Lord let my life be a blessing in Jesus name

Give thanks to the Lord and keep praising Him.

CHAPTER 3

CAN A CHRISTIAN BE POSSESSED?

Now that you are free, go and free others, Now that you have the fire! Go and spread it. The more you give the more you receive. I am going to start addressing you as a minister not as the one that needs ministry. If you went through the first two chapters properly, then by now you know your stand and should start thinking as one who will minister deliverance to others. In this chapter I want to deal with a very sensitive issue and I promise you after this you will have clarity and understanding. Now here is the big question going on in the Church of Jesus Christ;

"Can a born again Christian be demon possessed?"

What do you think? Before you say much let me explain something's very important. Note the question is asking about possession, which literally means total control or ownership. So I want to suggest to you that, let us first narrow down on these subject so we can understand it fully. Cause there is difference between being possessed and being demonized, but hold that thought; let me get to the word and give you the answers.

Allow me to first answer this question and give you some light on the question itself and its meaning. After much prayers and research from Scriptures and ministers I have discovered some great truths that will help us as the Church to put this subject to rest once and for all. Experience has taught us that born-again Christians do get sick and experience a lot of attacks that are demonic. I have personally prayed for believers who were saved and born-again but under attack from the enemy, some bound, depressed, some sick, either one way or the other it was clearly the work of the devil that kept them bound.

Most Christians that ague against Christians being demonized maintain the idea that the Spirit of God cannot dwell with an evil spirit. I will speak more about this idea later. But my question to them is how is it that so many professing Christians are bound and having some kind of demonic oppression. I am sure you know of a Christian that is experiencing what I am taking about. And it is not Gods will for them to be bound or oppressed but somehow the enemy is the one responsible.

POSSESSION VS DEMONISATION

Possession is total ownership of another, whereas demonization is demonic influence at varied levels. **I agree one hundred percent that a born again Christian cannot be possessed by a demon. The notion of a Christian being demon possessed doesn't appear anywhere in the New Testament**. The word used in the Bible is the Greek word *demonizomai* meaning demonized or having a demon. Jesus cast out demons from people who had them, people whom we say were possessed of the demons, but of Christians we do not hear any that were possessed, because demonic possession is impossible for truly born-again Christians. **If I possess something I own it. And the devil doesn't own Christian they belong to God**. So rest assured if you have accepted Jesus Christ as your Lord and Savior you cannot be demon possessed, but you can be demonized, meaning through open doors that you allow the devil to gain access into your life to the point that he will influence you and eventually control you. There are Christians out there that have allowed the devil to use them. Jesus never meant for anyone to be demonized or possessed, its people who choose to be bound, sometimes these spirits operate through our families, but you and I have a choice to stand up and break the curse or to allow the devil to use us.

YOU WERE BOUGHT BACK

The word which graphically explains salvation is the word, redeemed; literally meaning 'bought back' this means you were once in God and when man sinned the devil took ownership of you and me. That is why Jesus had to come, but not only that, but to pay a price through the shedding of His blood on the cross, so you can be reconciled to God or re-possessed to Him.
You that are born again you were bought back or redeemed. You once belonged to the devil but now you belong to God. This is a very powerful

truth that should set you free. The Blood of Jesus paid in full for your life and the devil is not your lord anymore. Now at this point I want you to declare your Deliverance through the blood of Jesus: say these prayers out loud:

- ➢ I declare that I belong to God and the devil cannot touch me in Jesus name and by the blood of Jesus.
- ➢ Jesus paid for my redemption in full; I refuse to be the devils playground.
- ➢ Any area that the devil still has ownership upon my life I claim it back now by the blood of Jesus.
- ➢ I disconnect from every evil ties with the kingdom of darkness and uproot and scatter their foundations in Jesus name and by the blood of Jesus.
- ➢ I have been bought back from the hands of the enemy and God now possess me in Jesus name and by the blood of Jesus.

YOU ARE LIKE A HOUSE THAT IS BEEN BOUGHT

This illustration below is by far the best I have discovered in clarifying this issue of demonization and Christians. Now imagine you have bought a house and the land it stands on, but this house once belonged to a foreigner who didn't take good care of it. The fact that you bought the house doesn't change the fact that it has defects that need to be fixed. Maybe you might have to change the roof, the window frames etc. That is how the conversion process takes place. Especially for people who get born again later in life, there are things that the Lord has to deal with and fix. It's not an automatic process. The owner being you has to now allow God to get to work; this is the sanctification process of the Holy Ghost. **And the battle for ownership starts. As the Holy Spirit must dispossess any illegal occupants that might still be on your piece of land that the previous owner left behind.** There could be some woodworms that need to be destroyed. At that moment a pest control company will have to come and to remove unwelcomed occupants. If you being the owner ignore the woodworms, they will eat up all the wood and roof until the house is in worst state. That is exactly what the demons do. If left unchecked or removed they take possession and invite more demons to come and destroy. This is why you will hear of someone who was once born-again but backslide and ends up in worst state than before.

A teacher I once knew was rebuked to stop dating a school girl he was teaching in his class. This teacher was a pastor. He became rebellious and didn't want to listen to the rebuke. He argued that he liked the girl despite the fact that she was under age and his student. He was a powerful young upcoming pastor; he had just been to a theological school and God was using him. He chose to let the devil deceive him and decided to quit; he left not only the school, but the church and eventually God. He ended up back to where he came from, smoking and drinking and was completely lost. Now this is how the devil works and destroys the children of God. Is your house safe, are you constantly under Gods leading and protection. The enemy will try always to invade your life, but you have to keep him out. Jesus is your owner and the devil has no right.

YOU ARE A TARGET

Remember that the devil interest and focus is the born-again children of God. He has come to kill, steal and destroy. And his assignment is to steal Gods people away from God; the Bible calls him the accuser of the brethren. When meetings are held in the underworld, the devil's message is clear regarding Christians; his message is to attack Christians. He is quoted at times by former Satanists as saying to his assembly; "We should only fight the real Christians **my time is near, therefore "we should fight as never before and make sure no one enters 'that place (heaven)'."**
He continued and he said that; since man likes flashy and fancy things, he would continue to manufacture these things and make sure that man has no time for his God and that he would use the following to destroy the church:
1. Money
2. Wealth
3. Women

Let's take time and bring the devil to his knees now; declare as follows at the top of your voice;

> I declare the name of JESUS upon every meeting and assembly from the kingdom of darkness.
> I declare that the every knee bows and tongue confesses that Jesus Christ is Lord.
> Devil I command you and all your agents to bow in the name of Jesus Christ of Nazareth.
> I destroy every plan the devil has against my life and my church now by fire in Jesus name; I scatter all your plans and meetings.
> I break the curse of poverty, fornication and pride upon my life.
> I sent back now by fire every evil and false gifts that you have channeled to my life and the saints to deceive us in Jesus name.
> I call down fire now upon the enemy's camp and declare no weapon formed against me shall prosper in Jesus name.

You are covered and protected by God, like the house that's been bought there is now new ownership. But you have to guard your heart and mind, guard against sin and keep your land under Gods ownership. This way the devil will not have access into your house.

JESUS PRACTICED DELIVERANCE

Jesus never said to his disciples that after people have responded to the gospel that all demons pack their bags and go. He also never said all born-again Christians have demons. Remember at this stage we have answered the question of Christian being possessed, and we said no! Christian cannot be possessed, but they can be demonized or influenced by demons. When Jesus sent out the disciples he commanded them to preach the gospel and cast out demons. That is what the Bible teaches and yes it was before Pentecost, but remember the great commission in Matthew 28: 19-20 that Jesus commanded us; He said do exactly as I did, which included deliverance. So both the Christians before Pentecost and after are to follow this command. The blood of Jesus is sufficient, Jesus did the finished work. There are people that receive Christ and immediately are delivered as I wrote in the first chapter that deliverance is part of Salvation. But there are also people that need deliverance and normally it is either these demons didn't leave them at

conversion or due to open doors the demons come back to their former home or they laid hidden deep in them. People experience salvation in different ways and that doesn't mean if you get saved and still have some bondage that you will not go to heaven when Jesus comes. No!
I personally had instant deliverance from smoking and drinking on the day I accepted Christ, but I had friends who still struggled with the habit of smoking. They received the same prayer as I did, but they didn't have deliverance in all areas. I believe Gods word is a word of deliverance, the Bible says; He sent His word and healed all our diseases. **Deliverance is guaranteed for Gods people, it might be instant or take time, but the most important is for Gods people to know the truth.** And the truth sets you free. It's time to discern in our lives and identify where we are. Total Freedom in Christ is our standard, abundant life is our portion. Anything short should make us restless. God responds to faith. You don't have to wait until Jesus comes to be free. Today you can decide to want your freedom and God can give it to you. Know Him, know His word and all things are possible to those who believe.

CAN A CHRISTIAN HAVE A DEMON? LET'S SEE FROM THE BIBLE

Yes of course Christians can have demons and in actual fact they can even invite more demons into their lives through ignorance and sin. This is called *daimonizomai* meaning demonized; Let me give you an example of what I mean. **In Mathew 16:13-23 Jesus speaks to His disciples** *and asked them who do you say I am? Some answered and said to him some say you are John the Baptist some say you are Elijah and others say you are Jeremiah or one of the prophets.*
But He said to them, 'who do you say that I am';
Peter answered and said; 'You are Christ the Son of the living God'. Jesus replies to him as says, Blessed are you Simon Bar-Jonah for flesh and blood has not revealed this to you, but My father who is in heaven.' This is a good confession from Jesus and shows that Peter was in the Spirit to be able to discern from the Father.
Not long Jesus began to speak to them about His death on the cross, how He will suffer and be killed and be raised on the third day. And Peter, who was

very much in the Spirit earlier, takes Jesus to the side and begins to rebuke Jesus, and say; *'far it be from you Lord; this shall not happen to you:'*
Jesus turned and said to Him; **'Get behind me Satan, you are an offence to Me, for you not mindful of the things of God, but of man.**
Now this is a perfect example to what the devil does to Christians. In the next chapter I speak about levels of Demonic manifestations. The devil can demonize Spirit filled Christians, he did to Peter he can do it to you.
Let's make a prayer before we go further, I sense the Spirit of God, wants you to be aware of this and not to assume that all your thoughts are from God, you and I will experience this kind of demonization and should be armed to deal with it;
When you feel a thought coming to you that is contrary to the will of God, a strange or evil thought deal with it immediately; I recommend this prayer which must be said out load;

> ➢ **Devil and all your lying demons, I cast you out of my mind now in Jesus name.**

Sometimes you may have to repeat it several times until he flees. The Bible teaches that resisting the devil will make him flee. Remember the devil is got no power over you, he can't control because you are born again, you belong to God, and so you are in charge. Demons attack your mind through fiery arrows or demonic thoughts. Be watchful as this is; it is often the entry point for demons.

People have long history of demonic oppression, most people have suffered rejection and past hurts. Often this are spiritual issues that as soon as a person is born again, this spirits must be dealt with, there should be deliverance prayers made either while you leading the person to the Lord or prayer afterwards. So as to make sure a person is fully set free. Depend on the Spirit of God to lead you.

HOW CAN AN EVIL SPIRIT AND HOLY SPIRIT DWELL WITHIN THE SAME PERSON AT THE SAME TIME?

This is a very good question which I want to answer here so as to help us further understand this chapter. It is true that the Bible teaches that light and darkness cannot dwell together. We all agree that the Spirit of God cannot dwell together with the evil spirit, but think about this; how could Jesus who was sinless and being God come into a sinful world filled with demonic influence. The only reason I believe the Son of man could come to such an evil planet is summed up in John 3:16, *For God so loved the world that he sent His one and only begotten son that whoever believes in Him will not die but have eternal life.*

How was that possible? You say? Because of love, God despite the sin and evil on this planet, He still sent Jesus to live in it. The Love made Him to endure all the shame, the cruel soldiers, the mocking, the nails that drove Him to the cross. It was the eternal love of God, which we humans cannot comprehend, but God is Love; He is that amazing!

So yes the Spirit of God cannot dwell with an unclean spirit, but they can co-exist in one body, just as Jesus could live in this evil world, so the Holy Spirit out of love can live inside a Christian, whilst they are demonized in some way or the other.

He the Holy Ghost is there to bring about sanctification and will not quit, as long as a child of God keeps their commitment to God. They will have God deliver them, heal them and restore them eventually.

> ➤ I declare total deliverance and restoration upon your life in Jesus name, any areas that the devil still has hold upon you, I declare that you are free now in Jesus name. May He create in you a clean heart and renew the right spirit within you, May he cast you not away from His presence and restore unto you the joy of your salvation, upholding you by His generous Spirit.

A WORD FOR THE CURSE BREAKERS

'I want you at this point to let you know that; you are the curse breaker; yes that's why God saved you in your family for this purpose. Jesus has raised you to change your family history. You are learning all this truths because God wants you to be equipped and armed. You are the one that should lead the way in your family. You carry a peculiar anointing. What you say is very important. Your prayers matter to God and your calling is very important to God. A curse breaker knows who they are, may God reveal to you, your ministry and role you need to play. This is a season for you to emerge and to be a vehicle of Gods

blessings into your family. Curse breakers in this season will not only affect families but communities, countries and nations will be impacted by them.'

In closing this section let me tell you a short story about my mom; God raised her to be a first generation curse breaker in our family. My grandmother from my mother's side was under the spirit of divination she was bound by water spirits and ancestral worship. She was a devoted member of one of the marine (water spirit) cults in our country; we called them *mathuela* in sotho. I can remember as a small boy how my grandmother will wear white beads and be so committed to her faith. Not long she passed on and my mother had been saved earlier in her twenties. I was told that when I was born there were ropes and beads placed on my hands and feet and waist. Somehow the curse breaker anointing on my mother compelled her to take a scissor and to cut off these ropes. She changed the destiny of her family. Everyone after her feared God, Jesus Christ became the deliverer of our family. Years went past and God through her prayers brought her husband, my father to Christ. My family has experience God's blessing and favor since then. I am second generation Curse breaker and the task is huge, but by the grace of God we will get to where God wants us to be. That is to impact our families and nations; to see them saved and living a godly life for Gods glory.

IN CONCLUTION

Jesus has died on the cross for you and for me. Let's take our rightful place; **I am not in any way suggesting in this chapter that every Christian has a demon, because there are those who teach such doctrines.** You can be free and be completely immune from demonic manifestations, but there will be times when the enemy tries to attack you, or influence you, remember you are no dwelling place for demons, keep your live pure before God. The enemy is stubborn and will keep coming. **You cannot stop the birds of the air from flying above your head, but you can stop them from building a nest on top of your head.** Any signs of demonic influence or oppression address them immediately. Any unconfessed areas of past hurts or rejection, deal with them. Know the fruits of the Spirit and discern your motives and heart. Do not be confused God promised freedom and freedom is what you have. Open doors and legal grounds are to be dealt with, so we can be free to serve our God.

PRAYERS AND FASTING CHAPTER 3

Now that we have dealt with this area, I need you to spend time, preferably a day asking God to reveal to you anything in your life that is not pleasing to Him.
This will be accompanied by fasting (water only fast) for a day. As you do a self-introspection, the Spirit will bring to the surfaces areas you have ignored or left unattended. For some it will be unforgiveness, rejection, bitterness, perhaps you struggle to submit to God or authority, there are people saved that are still held back in so many areas. So deal with them. Pray to God to heal, deliver and restore you. He might show you a picture of someone you have hurt or have not forgiven; confess and if you have to go and make right with your brother or sister go.

Read Psalms 51 and meditate on it.
The Lord is going to do the rest as the Spirit leads you.

CHAPTER 4

THREE KINDS OF DEMONIC MANIFESTATION

KNOW GOD, KNOW YOURSELF AND KNOW YOUR ENEMIES
In this chapter we are about to learn a very important area in deliverance. The devil is a cunning creature and will always try and find ways to oppress Gods people, but in the name of Jesus he is subject to us. We are the once who should keep him under our feet. I believe the number one area we should focus on as the 21st century church is to know who our God is, who we are and lastly who is our enemy. **The more we know him the more we know us. The more we know ourselves the more our enemies are terrified of us.** Ignorance is one of the weapons of the devil and God speaking of His people not the world, but His own; and He says My people perish for lack of knowledge. This scripture always challenges me and I will quote it until Jesus comes. For myself and my brothers and sister, we don't have to know everything, but if you can focus on these three things know them well and in this order, you will advance in life and God will honor your faith. They are once again; 1) know God 2) know yourself and 3) lastly know your enemies. We wrestling not against flesh and blood but, against principalities, against powers, against rulers of darkness of this age, against spiritual hosts of wickedness in heavenly places, therefore take up the whole armor of God so that you may be able to withstand in the evil day, and having done all to stand. Ephesians 6:12-13
Whatever the level you find yourself, some of you might still be having some form of oppression or obsession as you will learn in this chapter. I urge you to stand your ground. And resist the enemy, he will flee.
Know Lets pray this prayer before we proceed.

- ➢ Lord I pray in Jesus name let me grow in the knowledge of You.
- ➢ Lord I ask in Jesus name let me know who I am in Christ Jesus.
- ➢ Lord let me not be blinded to see my enemies, expose them in Jesus name.

Chapter 3 and 4 are very similar and give a lot insight into Christianity and demonization, so before you go further with this chapter make sure you have read and understand chapter 3.

THREE KINDS OF DEMONIC MANIFESTATION

I like to use this illustration to explain the three levels of demonic manifestation. Picture this with me, it's like a demon that comes and sits on your shoulder he is a mini demon and he stands in length from your shoulder to ear that's how tall they are. He begins to whisper into your ears all the time. He bosses you around, he is small so you sometimes boss him too, but since he is always talking to you, you end up believing his lies. **As you believe his lies the more he grows. He is totally depended on you; you agree with him he grows until he is tall over your head and eventual big enough to carry you.** He decides one day since he is big and you are his servant, now after all those obedient acts you did for him, now it's time to switch places. You now diminished to a mini he puts on his shoulder and the demon carries you around. He is taken full control of you. This are the three levels in an illustrative way. Where are you now in your life? Is there a demon ordering you around? Making you angry? Bitter? Unforgiving? Lustful? Greedy? Or are you carried around bound in an addiction that you can't get out of? Carried around by demons to do their will. Or are you free, no demon on your shoulder, you walking in the will of your father. The choice is yours

Here are the levels;

1. OPPRESSION

2. OBSESSION

3. POSSESSION

1. What does it mean to be spiritually oppressed?

> ➢ To oppress means to bear down, come against, or bind from the outside by a force greater than you.

- To oppress, is to afflict with certain spirits that are beyond your control.

- To oppress means to be weighed down, or be under a yoke and a heavy burden. This oppression is accomplished by evil spirits in various ways. They cause depression, create negative circumstances, and insert wrong thoughts into the mind such as thoughts of suicide, immorality, unbelief, fear, etc. This thoughts or emotions are what the Bible calls fiery darts, they are arrows projected against your mind to oppress you. **For the devil to oppress someone they will have to gain access through some means it can be an evil dream, exchange of gifts, lying on of hands, consulting ungodly mediums**. Do you have experiences where you acted outside you normal self? I have seen people who were very honest and God fearing doing things that are not of God, why? It's the spirit of oppression.

The spirit of Oppression does not live inside a man, but is an outside influence from the spirit realm. These projections can come via families too, meaning inherited. There are families that are entrenched in poverty everyone in that family never makes it. There are all kinds of generation oppression that gets passed on; this is a result of this spirit of oppression.

Kinds of oppression can include;

- Bodily oppression
- Physical oppression
- Mental oppression
- Spiritual oppression
- Financial oppression

How do we break the backbone of oppression? By spiritual warfare. Identify the areas the enemy is oppressing your life and let's call upon the Holy Ghost fire to deal with them. Pray violently these prayers the Bible says oppression makes a wise man mad in Ecclesiastes 7:7. Before it's too late lets break this spirit in your life;

- Holy Ghost fire Come upon me know in Jesus name

- Every inherent domestic oppression from my family's house assigned to ruin my life catch fire now and die in Jesus name.

- Every dream oppression agents assigned over me, I command you to scatter by fire in Jesus name.

- I fire back every arrow of oppression in the name of Jesus.

- (Lay your hand on your stomach) Every serpent sent to destroy me I command it to catch fire now. (Repeat this prayer as you touch your head as well)

- Every spirit of poverty that is sent upon my life I command you to catch fire and die in Jesus name.

- Poverty you are not my portion, sickness you are not my portion, oppression you are not my portion in Jesus name.

- Spirit of sickness and infirmity I command you to leave me; I shall live and not die to declare the glory of the Lord.

I receive from the Lord because His word is true and cannot lie; *"How God anointed Jesus of Nazareth with the Holy Ghost and with power: who went about doing good, and healing all that were oppressed of the devil; for God was with Him."* **(Acts 10:38)**

2. What does it mean to be spiritually obsessed?

- Obsession means a form of spiritual bondage which makes one addicted to a certain thing.

All bad addiction is a manifestation of this spirit. There are people no matter how hard they try; they will always fall back to the same addictions. This level of demonic manifestation is a compelling force that makes you do something that you know it's wrong, but you still do it. The obsessive spirits is to make you unclean. This form of demonic activity is very popular in the house of God. Whenever you find yourself compromising on your holiness towards God, know for sure there is an obsessive spirit tempting you to sin all the time. I appeal to men and woman of God out there lets teach our people about this. No child of God is expected to live an unholy life. All of us are called to holy living, obsessive spirits loves to entice Gods people with temporary, fleshly pleasures and unless one is prayerful and fasts a lot this spirits often take advantage of the flesh. **The stronger your flesh is, the more likely you will be obsessed.**

Obsession is also a control type spirit that takes advantage of the lack of knowledge of man. The devil's aim with the spirit of obsession is to disconnect men from heaven, by leading them into unholy living.

Let's heed the warning in Revelation 21:7-8 that says; *He that overcomes shall inherit all things; and I will be His God and he shall be My son. But the fearful, and unbelieving, and the abominable and murderers and whoremongers, and sorcerers, and idolaters, and all liars, shall have their part in the lake which burns with fire and brimstone: which is the second death.*

Saints of God hell is real and was never meant for born again children of God, Let us take our spiritual life seriously, live a holy life at all costs.

Know it's time to confront obsession (if you have an area that is not surrendered to Jesus, a habit that you want to part with take this opportunity to deal with it)

> ➢ Every devil in the form of obsession programmed to destroy my destiny I command you to live me now in Jesus name.

> ➢ (mention all negative habits that you have) and renounce each one of them; Lord Jesus I renounce…………………..(e.g. stealing) in the name of Jesus, Lord forgive me for not honoring your Word. I declare………………………(stealing) is not my portion and from today I receive my deliverance in Jesus name.

> ➢ Every obsession sent to destroy my finances and put me in debt, I command you to catch fire and die in Jesus name.

- ➢ Any witchcraft projection to obsessively put evil thoughts and patterns in my life, I destroy you in Jesus name.

- ➢ I put on the helmet of salvation now in Jesus name, any thought not of God be exposed and destroyed.

- ➢ I call upon the Holy Ghost fire to destroy the covenant of obsession in my life

- ➢ Any demonic delaying spirits upon my plans be destroyed by fire in Jesus name.

- ➢ I command a free life, a free mind, a mind of Christ and the fruits of the Holy Spirit to be my portion in Jesus name it is done. Amen.

3. What does it mean to be spiritually possessed?

Demons or evil spirits or even Satan himself can also possess human beings. Demonic possession is a condition in which one or more evil spirits inhabit the body of a human being and take complete control of their victim at will. They exercise authority over them. The only thing left is the person's personality. And the victim is subject to them. Possession does not mean a person is not responsible for his own sin. He is responsible and often he would have been deceived and led into that state.

As in the case of Satanists or devil worshippers possession can happen willingly. A person may desire to be taken over by spirit powers in order to push the devils agenda, pronounce curses, become a witch, or secure some other supernatural power. Possession can also occur unwilling. An individual does not ask to be possessed, but through sinful thoughts, actions, or contact with the occult, possession may result.

The evil spirit will use the physical body of their victim to carry out all their demonic activities, until such a time that the spirit is cast out, the person will continue until the devil destroy them completely.
Remember the story in Mark 5: 1-5 of a man who lived in tombs who had an unclean spirit. The Bible says no one could bind him, not even with chains,

because he would pull them apart and break them in pieces. This is clearly unnatural.

Demonic possession separates people from society, it destroys their dignity, and one can even behave like an animal. Because the devil wants to make a mockery of God's creation.

Any person who is fully under the control of the evil spirits needs prayer; the Lord can still save them. Do you know someone like that? Do not take it lightly. Make time to fast and pray for you or whoever is under this possession. Find a pastor or believers that can pray with you. With man it is impossible but with God all things are possible.

HOW DEMONS OPERATE

Demons are agents of Lucifer called Satan and their main mission is to oppose God, His plans and purposes, and His people. They also war against unbelievers to keep them from the truth of the Gospel. They are after the destinies of men especially in marriages, ministries, business, child bearing, finances etc. The devil will stop at nothing to fight the saints in this areas, His agenda is to kill, to steal and to destroy. **Demons operate through families or control of specific territories also known as principalities** such as the prince of Persia mentioned in Daniel 10:12-13.there is areas that are known and famous for specific things, such as crime, prostitution, witchcraft. Such areas are under the blanket of demonic influence. Demons also work through personalities or through men and women to accomplish satanic missions in the world. There are people who worship Satan and are used in the kingdom of darkness.

Opposition to God's will is Satan's main agenda. The word "Satan" means "adversary." Satan is primarily God's adversary see Job 1:6; Matthew 13:39. He is secondarily, man's adversary see Zechariah 3:1; I Peter 5:8.

Demons have different natures. There are thousands of them, with different characters. One demon identified himself in 1 Kings 22:23 as a "lying spirit." A "deaf and dumb" spirit is identified in Mark 9:25. Demons of various natures operate as spirits of infirmity, seducing spirits, and unclean spirits. Satan uses them to war against peoples in body, soul, and spirit.

WHAT IS THE SPIRITS OF INFIRMITY AND HOW IT OPERATES

These are spirits that afflict the bodies of believers as well as unbelievers. A lot of Christians are attacked in this area. There are sicknesses that are evil in nature. Infirmities can include grief, sorrow, pain or distress. They are not necessarily sickness but they open a door to sicknesses. For example bitterness can lead to cancer. These sicknesses are masterminded by the devil, they are from the underworld. Doctors will call them arthritis or slipped disc or cancer. But Jesus called it a spirit of infirmity. It's not right for a child of God to get sick imagine this woman called a daughter of Abraham, in Luke 13:10-17. This woman was afflicted with a spirit of infirmity. She was attending a service on the Sabbath and Jesus called her "a daughter of Abraham." So she was a church goer and a covenant daughter of God of Israel, yet her body had been afflicted by Satan for eighteen years.

> Every spirit of infirmity assigned against your life, I rebuke it know in Jesus name. Just because your mother had it does not mean you have to have it. In Jesus name I command it to leave your body now.

Pray earnestly against spirit of unforgivess if you have, spirit of discouragement, bitterness, rejection, self-pity anything that does not resemble the fruits of the Holy Spirit resist it because the devil will use it to make you sick.

WHAT ARE SEDUCING SPIRITS

These spirits afflict the spirit of man, believer and non-believer seducing them to believe doctrinal lies and be condemned to eternal punishment. They are spirits of false doctrine, cults, false Christ, and false teachers or prophets. Be careful of where you fellowship. Be careful of what you read. Seducing spirits are everywhere the Bible says:

Now the Spirit speaketh expressly, that in the latter times some shall depart from the faith, giving heed to seducing spirits, and doctrines of devils. (1 Timothy 4:1)

These seducing spirits are deceptive. They actually work miracles which led some to believe they are of God. A lot of Churches are used by the devil in this area. We should be careful; Jesus said you will know them by their fruit. Jesus came to save man and not to give man miracle after miracle. Seek the God of miracles and not the miracles.

For they are the spirits of devils, working miracles, which go forth unto the kings of the earth and of the whole world, to gather them to the battle of that great day of God Almighty. **(Revelation 16:14)**

The Bible is clear that the devil can work miracles; yes he can, so we do not measure godliness by miracles but by the Spirit of truth. The Holy Ghost lives in you, may He lead you into all truth. And may you find a born again, Spirit filled house of God. That promotes the kingdom of God, That is truly leading man into heaven.

Seducing spirits can also include the "spirit of divination" mentioned in Acts 16:16;

"And it came to pass, as we went to prayer, a certain damsel possessed with a spirit of divination met us, which brought her masters much gain by soothsaying." **(Acts 16:16)**

Such spirits of divination or "familiar spirits" operate in fortune tellers, witches, or sangomas (witch doctor) and palm, crystal ball, and tea leaf readers use this spirit. Through demonic means, these spirits of divination foretell the future or things naturally unknown. Warnings against familiar spirits are given in Leviticus 19:31; 20:6; Deuteronomy 5:9; 18:10. Seducing spirits sear the conscience, seduce man, entice you, tempt you, and allure you into their trap until you are deceived. Seducing spirits are active in causing "spiritual wickedness in high places they operate over nations and large peoples groups." They are present and operative in every cult and wherever doctrinal error exists. Remember that Satan wants to be worshiped and he will take it any way he can get it.

WHAT ABOUT UNCLEAN SPIRITS

These demonic powers afflict the soul of man. They are responsible for all immoral acts, unclean thoughts, temptations and other strategies of Satan used to bind men and women in their soul or mind, will and emotions. When Satan oppresses peoples with unclean spirits, he can operate in their homes, churches, and entire nations as these groups are composed of individuals. This is how Satan works in the various levels of structure in society. For examples of unclean spirits see Matthew 10:1; 12:43.

HOW DEMONS GAIN CONTROL

He who digs a pit will fall into it, and whoever breaks a wall will be bitten by a serpent. Ecclesiastes 10:8

Demons gain control in several ways, remember the devil is very old and has masterminded ways to infiltrate man, the only weapon we have to stop him is the word of God. Here is briefly some of the ways he gains access and eventual control man.

   1. **Through generations:** Demons may oppress or possess a person because of previous possession or oppression of the parents. This explains why there are generational curses. This form of demonic influence over children and generations is found in (Exodus 20:5; 34:7; Deuteronomy 5:9).

   2. **Through the mind:** The mind is one of the major battlefields of Satan. The mind is the quickest way the devil can gain access. To reach your mind is easy; it's through what you hear or see. If Satan controls your thoughts, he will eventually control your actions. Lack of mental control eventually results in lack of use of the will. The Lord wants us to be so sensitive to our daily thoughts that we are able to distinguish when it's us, or when it's the devil talking. You fail to control you thoughts you will end up in sin. Continuing in sinful thoughts and actions will lead you from obsession to oppression and eventually possession. **Never empty your mind, that's demonic**

meditation and will open your life to astral projection and Satanism.

3. **Through sinful actions:** Sinful thoughts are fulfilled by sinful actions. For example, the thought of sexual immorality is fulfilled in the actual act of sexual intercourse. Sin is rebellion towards God, and rebellious thoughts and actions provide an entry point for demonic activity.

When a born again child of God continues in sinful thoughts or actions they "give place" to the devil (Ephesians 4:27) which means more spiritual room is given for the operation of the enemy and guess what the devil will maximize the opportunity. **I often say in my preaching's; be ten steps ahead of your enemy. Meaning be pro-active; do not play in the enemy's camp lest you get bitten by the snake**. Be careful of indulging in any occulting practices, such as reading star signs, tarot cards, consulting the dead or water spirits, anything that is not of God stay away from it, you stick to the Bible and you'll be safe.

An unbeliever who lives a sinful life is open not only to oppression of demonic powers, but also possession. There is no neutral ground in spiritual warfare. You are either on the side of good or evil. You belong either to God or Satan. If you belong to Satan and have not been born again, then you are his to use as he wills to oppress you, or possess you as he wills.

4. **Through desire:** Some people ask Satan for demonic power to enable them to perform supernatural acts. Most Satanists are recruited through this means. People desires to have powers, people desires to have riches. There is even websites that are set up to entice people into Satanism. **The price is your soul and once they have your soul they will give all the riches but only to destroy you in the end.**

5. **Through an empty house:** Demons think that the body of the person they inhabit is their own house (Matthew 12:44). When a person who is delivered from demonic powers does not fill his house with the new birth experience and the infilling of the Holy Spirit,

reentry may occur. Many times I have seen people experience a mighty deliverance only to fall back into it, and get worse that before, why? They neglected to replace their temple. When God sent Moses to Pharoah He said to him you are to tell Pharoah to let my people go so that they may worship Me. **God called you out so He can bring you into His service.** Never be neutral, be radical for God, and feed on Him constantly.

May the Lord give you victory in this areas. I believe strongly that there is light coming to you. The devil is exposed, now take you deliverance and go and share it with others. **After this chapter the next step is for you to testify, share what the Lord is doing, and be a blessing to others by ministering to them.**

CHAPTER 5

HOW SATAN FIGHTS CHRISTIANS

The number one prime target of the devil is Christians, if you are born again you need to know this, the Devil hates you to the core, and he is a merciless destructive creature who hates your success. He knows he is destined for the bottomless pit and is working day and night to deceive many so he can go to burn in hell with them. In 2 Corinthians 4:3-4 he is called the god of this age, who has blinded the minds of unbelievers who are perishing. This Devil cannot be taken lightly. We as the called out ones should know how to fight against him and overcome him in Jesus name.

A MEETING FROM THE UNDERWORLD CONVENTION

Here is a narrative of what the devil meets about; this is to give you an idea of what is said about you and me that are Christians; *"Satan called a worldwide meeting of demons. In his opening speech he said; 'we can't keep Christians from going to church, we can't keep them from reading the Bible, we can't keep them from having an intimate relationship with their master. Every time they gain connection with their Savior our power over them is broken.*
So this is what we must do, let them go church, but during the week and as often as we can we must steal their time, so they don't have enough time to spend with Jesus. And this is how I want you to do it said the devil:
Distract them from connecting with their master! All throughout the day. The demons shouted and said how could we accomplish this.
The devil answered, by keeping them busy, tempt them to do the unnecessary things, occupy their minds. Make them to spend, spend and spend and borrow and borrow, keep them in debts.
Deceive the wives to work long hours and husbands to work 6 to 7 days a week, 10 -12 hours a day, so they can't afford their empty lifestyle.
Keep them from spending time with their family and children. Stimulate their minds so they cannot hear the still small voice. Keep their minds focused on TV DVDs worldly entertainment. This will jam their minds and break their

connection with God. Fill their coffee tables with magazines, newspapers fill their minds with news, flood their driving with billboards, their mail with junk mail, keep them on internet all day.

Keep the skinny beautiful models on magazines and book covers and TV shows so that husbands believe outward beauty is what is important, so as they can dislike their wives. Keep the wives too tired to love their husbands and to satisfy them sexually.

Give them Santa Claus to distract their children about the true meaning of Christmas and feed them Easter eggs to distract them from the truth about the death and resurrection of Christ.

And when they meet in churches to fellowship make them to be involved in gossiping and complaining, this will leave their conscience troubled.
Crowd their lives with so many things that they don't have time for God
It was a clear message; demons were ready to carry out their assignment. The Christians are not to preach the gospel, they must be self-absorbed and not care, time is running out said Satan go to work, keep them busy....B USY.'

This is what BUSY stands for
B- Being
U- Under
S- Satan
Y- Yoke

Do you find yourself too busy, perhaps with work demands or life in general, are you hardly having time for God. I am not here to judge you, but to caution you. The devil is got you on his hit list. He is going to push his mission until he wins. But you and I can stop him.
There is an anointing that removes burdens and destroys the yoke. It is here know for you to experience. Let's pray against these deceiving worldly spirit that's keeping you BUSY! According to Isaiah 10:27 that says '**It shall come to pass in that day that his burden will be taken away from your shoulder and his yoke from your neck, And the yoke will be destroyed because of the anointing oil.**'

Pray these prayers:
- I cover myself with the blood of Jesus.
- I confess my sin of being too busy for God.
- I stand against any power assigned to put me under demonic yoke.
- I pull down the strongholds erected against my progress in Jesus name.
- I take the shield of faith and quench every fiery dart against me in Jesus name.
- Lord infuse my blood with your anointing that will produce hunger for you.
- I reject every evil arrangement concerning my marriage, family and children in Jesus name.
- I sent the fire of God upon every assembly, assembled against me, I scatter their assignment by fire in Jesus name.
- I command them to fall for my sake
- No weapon formed against me shall prosper, my name will not be mentioned in their meetings and by fire I cancel their work.
- I receive grace to serve God and to stay connected to him in Jesus name, Amen.

HOW SATAN AND HIS AGENTS ATTACK THE CHRISTIANS

We (Christians) should bear in mind that this is a spiritual battle. **The first step in victory is to realize your problem is spiritual.** The Bible say we are not wrestling against flesh and blood but against principalities, against powers, against rulers of the darkness of this world, against spiritual wickedness in high places (Eph 6:12). Also 1 Peter 5:8 says; Be sober, be vigilant because your adversary the devil, walks around like a roaring lion seeking whom he may devour.

Knowing these facts, the Bible gives us seven weapons in Ephesians 6:11-18 to fight against the devil. These are:
1. Truth
2. Righteousness
3. Gospel of Peace
4. Faith
5. Helmet of Salvation

6. The Word of God
7. Praying without ceasing

With the whole armor of God on us, we are fully covered. The amour of God is not just a roman soldier amour no! Its Gods armor and has His power in it. It stands tall in the spirit realm its bright and invisible **it was designed for offense and not defense**. If used properly it works all the time, the Lord is raising His army and this is their armor. The devil is stolen the amour from Gods people, but no more. Jesus awaits you and me to take our stand in battle.

The Christians are being attacked in different ways because of the power they possess. They are such a powerful people that demonic power cannot change or tamper with. Anybody who wants to tamper with born again Christians is playing with fire and God will crush him/her, because the Christians are the apple of God's eye (Zechariah 2:8b). The Bible records that Greater is He that is in the Christians than he (the devil) that is in the world (1 John 4:4b) and that "The weapons of our warfare are not carnal, but mighty through God to the pulling down of strongholds. (2 Corinth 10:3-6) Also the Bible says that the Christians are seated in the heavenly places with Jesus far above principalities and powers. (Ephesians 1:19-23, 2:6). These few scriptures are enough to bring down a legion of demons and get the devil on his knees. **Whenever Christians pray or declare the word of God fire comes out of their mouth.**

THE PIT OF HELL

In the spirit world, everybody has a satanic pit before them. When you are a born again Christian, the power of God lifts you out of the pit where the devil has been marching on your head. And you are placed above his head, hence the scriptures say in Luke 10:19; we are given power to trample over snake sand scorpions and over all the power of the enemy. For the fact that you are now the sons of God (John 1:12) you are a terror to the devil and his kingdom. But the unbelievers are always in the pit where the devil is marching on their heads. God has given the Christians power, authority and dominion over the devil through His Son Jesus (Colossian 1:16-29, Luke

10:19, Mark 16:18a. So stand up and begin to march on the head of the devil because he belongs to the ground.

Take time now to walk around and trample over every devil and demons in Jesus Name and Declare:
- Praise to the Lord and shame to the devil.
- Satan I trample over you now in Jesus name;
- Poverty you are under my feet.
- Sickness you are under my feet.
- Lack you are under my feet.
- Fear you are under my feet.
- Debts you are under my feet.
- Generational curses you are under my feet.
- Depression you are under my feet.
- Unforgiveness you are under my feet.
- Bondage you are under my feet.

In Jesus Name (begin to trample literally and take your ground in the spirit)

TOO HOT TO HANDLE

The devil is confused with the type of power the Christians possess. To his computer the power of the Christians is 100% fire of God. They are too hot for him to handle. Remember the story of Shadrack, Meshach and Abednego; they were so hot that the fire could not burn them when they were thrown into a burning furnace. According to the devil, when the Christians are at such a very high degrees of Power and Fire of God, the power of the Holy Ghost in them is too much for him because they are usually fearful and horrible at such high frequency causing disaster to his wicked world. With such high degrees they are able to climb a slippery ladder in the spirit world that no demon can climb and can subdue wickedness in high and low places. They literally become invisible on the demonic rather. They are like the wind, they cannot be traced or seen where they come from and where they are going.

A Christian is only powerful when they pray (1 Thessalonians 5:17). A prayerless Christian is a powerless Christian. **A prayerless Christian looks very empty and cold to the kingdom of darkness.** Through prayers, the Christian can stop all satanic actions. The devil knows the power in prayer so; he tries all means to make the Christians powerless by sowing some spiritual tares into them so that they will find it difficult to pray fervently. Be careful of what you dream because it is often the time when the enemy steals your virtue and anointing. When such a Christian is no longer living up to expectations as a Christian they begin to fall into the satanic pit. The devil can then have access to them, oppress them and reduces the fire of God gradually.

One type of sowing through demonic dreams or attacks that the devil uses to Christians is the spirit of laziness accompanied with the spirit of fear. The Bible records in 2 Timothy 1:7 that God hath not given us the spirit of fear, but of power, and love and of a sound mind and in Romans 12:11 we are exhorted not to be slothful in business but fervent in spirit, serving the Lord.

HOW CHRISTIANS ARE KNOWN BY THE DEMONS?

The born again Christians **are known in the spirit world by the light that shines continuously like a very bright candle in the heart or a circle of light around the head or a wall of fire around them.** When a Christian is walking along, **demons see angels walking along with them, one by the right, one by the left, and one behind.** This makes it impossible for demons come near.

The only way demons can succeed to get to Christians is by making them to sin, thereby giving them a loophole to come in. When a Christian is driving a car and the demons want to harm them, they find that a Christian is never alone in the car. There is always an Angel by him or her. It still amazes the demons how Christian can sometimes be so powerless, if only they knew the power in them. **There is so much light and power you possess as a born again child of God, now it's the time to release it. Prayer releases that power.**

THE MAKING OF BACKSLIDDEN CHRISTIANS

Listen to this testimony from a former chairman of Lucifer himself;
 'As a chairman appointed by Lucifer, I would send beautiful women to living churches and fellowships. These women would be well dressed and after the preaching would come out for the altar call, pretend to have received Christ and would be prayed for. At the end of the fellowship or service they would hang around waiting for the preacher who naturally would be very happy for these new converts.
The said convert may even follow the preacher to his house. If the preacher does not have the spirit of discernment she would lure him into the sin of fornication or adultery. This takes place the moment he admires her lustfully. She would make sure he continued in this sin until she finally quenches the Spirit of God in him and then leave him, **mission accomplished**'.

Here is another similar story of a minister by the same chairman of Lucifer;
'This is a true story about a pastor. In the evil spirit world he is known as a man of God. When he went on his knees there would be confusion among us. We therefore sent young beautiful woman to him. This man would even feed them but would refuse to be enticed. They did all they could but never succeeded. As a result, these girls were killed for their failure.

I then changed to a woman and went to him, and by words and actions tried to entice him, but he was adamant. This was too much for me, so I decided to kill him physically. One day, this Minister went to the market. I watched him and as he bent down to price some commodities I wheeled an oncoming trailer loaded with drums of oil into the market where he was. The trailer struck the high tension pole and fell right into the market, leaving many people dead, but this Minister escaped. How he escaped was a miracle. Another day, I saw him travelling to town on foot. I again wheeled an oncoming army lorry loaded with yams to kill him. The lorry went straight into the cemetery road, killed many people, but this Minister again escaped. After this second attempt we gave up. He is still alive!'

Because of a single Christian, the devil may decide to destroy many souls, thinking he could kill them, but he always fails. These incidents had happened to many Christians unknown to them, **but their God always delivered them.** The trouble is, **the devil does not give up.** His thoughts are always: "I may succeed one day." But he never does. **As long as the Christian walks with God and in love and remains in Him and does not get entangled with the affairs of this life, the devil can never succeed, no matter how hard he tries.** Only the unbeliever is at his disposal.

THE OPPRESSION OF THE CHRISTIAN

As I stated that Christians cannot be possessed, but they can be oppressed or obsessed by the demons. This mostly happens in dreams. The Bible says in Matthew 13:25; while men slept his enemy came and sowed tares among the wheat and went his way. It is imperative for Christians to pray in the night, especially around 11pm - 3am. This is the time when the demons are at work and unless someone is standing in the gap, a lot of damage will be done.
A Christian may see in their dreams the following:

1. A dead relation visiting them.
2. People pursuing them.
3. See themselves swimming in the river.
4. Friends bringing food and asking them to eat.
5. Having sex with a known or unknown person.

These are dream attacks, I have a chapter on this subject and we will get more into details there. For now, watch your dreams. Any signs of attacks, seek deliverance. Having sexual intercourse in a dream if not dealt with, can sometimes leads to barrenness. Or a pregnant woman sees herself having sexual intercourse with a man, could also lead to a miscarriage.

Get into a habit of praying in the night, any attacks of this nature demands that you get up and rebuke the devil immediately. You don't wait. If they persist seek prayer support from your pastor.

THE DEVIL'S SOUL WINNING

When Jesus Christ was leaving this earth, He gave us all a great commission; *"Go ye into all world and make disciples of all nations."* While some Christians are still waiting for a more suitable and convenient time to do the great commission, the devil has also has given this commission to his agents. The difference between them and us is that, **the devil's agents are more serious in winning souls than the Christians!** They don't sleep and they are very committed.

Satan is a cunning creature, but he does not force anyone. What he does is to attract and make you come to him willingly. That is why the Bible says; "Resist the devil and he will flee from you" (James 4: 7).

DESTROYING CHURCHES

The devil goes to church, yes he does! Many churches have suffered, lost everything and closed down because of agents of darkness. The devil changes strategies, but in most cases he will sent an agent to go and spy out the church. They are in churches to study the weakness of the church. If the church is prayerless, these agents will be used to divide the church, they carry the spirit of Jezebel they entice men even the pastors of the church to fall. Sometimes if the pastor is strong they will use his wife. Demons will fight churches bring distractions and strife. They know the more the saints sin and fall into their trap the more they win.

Sometimes they will even be in leadership positions, and when given the pulpit they will release the spirit of Egypt. They will do everything in their power to destroy the house of God.

FASTING AND PRAYER CHAPTER 5

At this stage I will love you to remember you are being prayed for, you need not fear, this information is there to expose the devil and to give you and me the right knowledge so we know who we are dealing with.
I will love you now to fast 3days (Water only Fast) This FAST IS CALLED **THE YOKE BREAKING FAST**

THESE SET OF PRAYERS YOU WILL REPEAT THEM DAILY AND PREFARABLY IN THE NIGHT TIME HOURS 00h00-03h00

I believe it's your season to breakthrough in the spiritual realm and sometimes for us to see a change in our lives we must do what we never done before.

1. Father in the name of Jesus I destroy every yoke off my neck, I break it now in Jesus name.
2. In the name of Jesus I crush them with the rod of iron and dash them to pieces.
3. I destroy the arm of the wicked against my destiny.
4. I release myself from any inherited bondage in Jesus name.
5. O lord ordain a terrifying noise in the camp of my enemies.
6. Angels of God begin to hinder and stop every operation of darkness against my life.
7. I cast down every evil manipulation against my life, my family, pastor and church in Jesus name.
8. I cancel every accident planned against my life and loved ones in Jesus name.
9. I declare myself invisible to the powers of darkness, they will look for me but they will not find me.
10. I expose every evil witch or agent of darkness in my church, family or work; let them catch fire now in Jesus name.
11. I will not be enticed and lured by the spirit of Jezebel, I bind its power upon my life in Jesus name.
12. I decree this is my season to possess my possession and to take back everything the devil has stolen.

Begin to give thanks daily as the Lord does His work. The Lord showed me a picture of an Angel ready to move as I was writing these prayers. I believe they are ready for you to speak His word. Jesus is Lord and every knee will bow in heaven and on earth and under the sea.

The next chapter is one of my favorite subjects, yes they will bow under the sea too; get ready to join me as we explore the kingdom of darkness under the sea. This time around we are going to rain brimstone and fire upon this evil kingdom until we subdue and have dominion. Our riches are held there, marriages are held there, anyway let me leave all that to our next chapter. God bless you as you keep reading and praying. Amen

---

CHAPTER 6

DEALING WITH THE MARINE KINGDOM

EXPOSING THE KINGDOM, MY PERSONAL TESTIMONY

It was summer evening some months ago at the writing of this book, when the Lord gave me a dream that opened my eyes to the marine kingdom; in fact there were two dreams that I had. In the first dream I was showed a group of women about six in number they were assembled by the river side. As I looked closely they had khaki clothing and before my eyes they went into the river and formed a circle in the water. At this stage they were walking on top of water, then in the same circle they seemed to go under water, but half of their bodies were still outside water and the other half inside water, I was surprised by this action. As I looked they came out and suddenly as we passed by that river with a group of people there was stones coming from the hill top, as if they are falling from heaven against us, we run for cover. The dream ended.

In my second dream, I was walking by the sea, I believe it was a sea because it was large and I felt I was on top of the water, the fear of drowning came upon me since I am not a good swimmer especially on the deep sea, so I was scared as I was in the middle of this sea, suddenly I was immersed in the water, but to my surprise I didn't drown I could breathe in the water and I was suddenly at the floor of the sea. I then moved towards the mountain under the sea as I could tell there was something there more than just water and fish. I went towards the mountain and suddenly I saw as though I am on the outskirts of a city, like looking at a city from afar and hidden so that no one can see me. I saw from my hiding place a black van passing by carrying people at the back, this people were very strange, they resembled zombies, their faces were so wicked, cold and frightening. I saw their look as they looked towards my direction from the back of the van. I was lifted up somehow. There was what I think was a gate as I remember a security guard there, but I managed to lift up this man with me and drop him down, I can't make out the security part except that there was someone there at the gates of the city and I happened to have control over them.

These two dreams were both interpreted and they both exposed the kingdom under the sea, the marine kingdom. **The Lord since then has given me what I will like to call a go-ahead, for me to speak about this kingdom.** I am a preacher and a Bible scholar so I knew there was such a place but I could never really speak about it, until the Lord showed me and revealed to me that no assembly from the kingdom of the sea fashioned against His people shall prosper. As the first dream portrayed they assemble in the water and then, there was attacks from the heavens, but nothing harmed us. I took this as a promise for myself and the Church of Jesus Christ. The second dream simply was saying that the Lord is giving me a glimpse into the spiritual underworld. I will be able to see them and even overpower their gates. I intend to study more and pray more for more revelation of how we as the Church can gain victory over this wicked kingdom. **The message God gave me was that I must tell the church about my experiences, teach them about these marine kingdom and teach them to fight, not only in the heavens and on the earth but also to fight under the sea. A lot of the Christian community has done warfare on the upward and horizontal direction and have missed the headquarters where all the planning and organizing is done which is in the sea.** So in this chapter I am going to equip you to war in all direction so that you can taste victory from the marine powers that have manipulated your lives, marriages, families, finances, nation and the world.

WHAT ARE MARINE SPIRITS

Every spirit being living in the sea or under water is known as a marine spirit. Marine kingdom is the greatest kingdom of all evil demonic kingdoms. **Marine kingdom is the most wicked and well organized kingdom of darkness, above all the other evil kingdoms, that exits in the air, the land and outside this planet.** The headquarters of marine kingdom is located within India Sea. And the Queen of the India Sea is the head of marine kingdom. While, Queen of the coast is next in command and she resides within the Atlantic Ocean both are among the fallen evil forces from heaven before.

Revelations 17: 1 speaks about these fallen beings; known as the queen of the sea; *And one of the seven angels who had the seven bowls came and talked with me saying to me; Come I will show you the judgment of the* **great harlot who sits on many waters,** *with whom the kings of the earth committed fornication, and the inhabitants of the earth were made drunk with the water of her fornication.*

MARINE SPIRITS IN THE BIBLE

God created the world to exist in three spheres;
1. The heavens
2. The earth
3. The sea

In Genesis when God made man He said; 'Let us make man in our image and after our likeness and let them have dominion over the fish of the SEA, and over the fowl of the AIR, and over all the cattle, and over every creeping thing that creeps upon the EARTH. You can clearly see the three spheres or dimensions as I have emphasized them. **The sea, the air and the land**. When God gave Moses the commandments; look what He said in Exodus 20:3-4; Thou shall not have other gods before me. Thou shall not make unto thee any graven image or any likeness of anything that is in the heavens above, or that is in the earth beneath, or that is in the water under the earth. There you see the three strongholds or spheres. Ladies and gentlemen there are beings under the sea. The Bible speaks of the **kings of the earth** in Psalms 2:2; it speaks of the **Prince of the power of the air** in Ephesians 2:2, and the **queen of heaven** in Jerimiah 44:19 who is worshiped by burning incense. Then there is the **great sea monster called the Leviathan**, in Ezekiel 29: 1-3 he is referred to as the great dragon that lies in the mists of the river, which have said; my river is mine I own it and I have made it myself.' This was clearly a spirit that claimed to own the water. It is also referred to as Pharoah spirit inside the water.

Now let's do a few more scriptures then we can start to pray with understanding and authority, because now we know from scripture that indeed there are inhabitants under the sea. I am doing this because there are people who believe there is no such a thing as marine spirits. As the Bible is not plainly clear about this, but through study and the help of the Holy Ghost we are able to see that indeed there is a marine kingdom.

Isaiah 27:1 says about the Leviathan; *in that day the Lord with His sore and great sword shall punish Leviathan the piercing serpent, even leviathan that crooked serpent and he shall slay the dragon that is in the sea.* Now why will God want to destroy a fish? Leviathan is a sea creature, just like whales and sharks, why will God be so specific in saying I will destroy it. Because it is a spirit. It is the king of the marine kingdom. This is what we call the snake spirit. Ever heard of snake pastors, this is the spirit they use to push the agenda of Satan.

In revelations 12:12 the Bible says; *therefore rejoice, ye heavens and ye that dwell in them. Woe to the inhabitants of the earth and of the sea, for the devil is come down unto you, having great wrath, knowing that he hath but a short time.*

There are inhabitants under the sea. The many testimonies of people who have been exposed to this world are true and biblical. Job 26:5 says **the dead tremble, those under the water and those inhabiting them.** Now I know why I saw zombies there. There are presumed dead people living under the sea. Witchcraft is one of the practices from this realm.

The devil has built a powerbase in the waters and his secretariat is in the heavens where the principalities supervise satanic oppression over people, territories, cities and nations.

Since the earth is founded upon the waters according to Psalms 104:5-5 and Gods throne is upon the waters (Psalms 29:3, 10) the devil who is a copycat decided to copy God and established his throne also in the waters. The marine kingdom is one of the least understood of the three spheres and the most powerful of them.

Thank God that we have been given dominion over all three kingdoms, the air, the earth and water. This authority is being restored upon the Church and God is using His sons and daughters to make the kingdoms of the world, to be the kingdoms of our God and His Christ.

WHY MARINE SPIRITS ARE SO POWERFUL

When you read from Genesis when God created the heavens and the earth there is a very interesting scripture there. In Genesis 1:6-8 we read about the separation of the firmament God dividing the waters above from the waters beneath. So it means there was water on top and below and God used the firmament to divide them. In Verse 9-10 God said; Let the waters under the heaven be gathered together until one place, and let the dry land appear; and it was so. And God called the dry land earth and the gathering of the waters called the seas; and God saw that it was good. God commanded the dry land to appear and commanded the waters to move one side so as the dry land can appear. This shows you that everything is from water. In fact humans are 70% water in volume. The planet we live in is 72% water. Water is everywhere and man and everything needs water to survive. The whole world is founded upon water the Bible says.

Now back to Genesis in verse 6-8 when God finished His work on the second day the Bible did not record that he said it was good. God did not say anything after he had separated the waters above and under, nothing said if there will be good or bad. I believe these is one of the ways we can see how God viewed these spheres. God loves the fish and he created it, nothing wrong with the sea and rivers, but we taking about the spiritual entity here the Lords creation should be enjoyed, I need to say this because I don't want you to stop loving water. It's a spiritual world we talking about here.

At the age of 14, Mrs Lena Ofosu was brought by her mother to a witchdoctor in Ghana. Little did she know that this witchdoctor was about to reveal to her mother that she had been chosen before birth to be the 'wife' of a demonic spirit from under the water and thus would have to undergo training to know how to perform ritual sacrifices to enable this 'spiritual husband' to meet and interact with her both in the spiritual and physical worlds.

Her confession after her remarkable deliverance at one of Gods houses is an eye-opener and one from which many lessons can be learned. These testimonies aren't meant to cause fear or give unnecessary attention to Satan but rather as a means of educating people about the reality of the spiritual world and the need for us to involve God in each and every single step we take.

The Underwater Kingdom of Satan

Demons who reside beneath the waters are called "Aquarius spirits" or "Marine spirits". These Demons are contacted only through witchcraft as to receive supernatural powers.

Their marine kingdom (which is spiritual) is established under the ocean and the headquarters of marine kingdom of Satan is said to be located beneath India's sea. The "queen of India Sea" is the head of marine kingdom, while the "queen of the coast" is next in command and resides within the Atlantic Ocean. It is said that both are also among the fallen angels.

The Marine kingdom of Satan is a highly organized and strategized place where high technological equipment's are used by high ranking Satanists who are psychiatrists and scientists, who work in labs tirelessly to design beautiful but seductive things. The things that are designed in that spirit world are said *to be latest weapons, perfumes, assorted types of cosmetics, flashy cars, different designs of electronics, etc.*

Many perfumes are made to lure men and women. Underwear's and sexy clothing to seduce and distract men are also made there. These things are used on earth to supply people who have signed a contract with Satan — sale and prosperity for a soul in return. These things are also given to most of the workers of the Occult for the sole purpose to distract people from Jesus Christ.

God promised me as you pray this prayers; just as the fire of God fell on mount Carmel in 1 Kings 18: 38 when the God of Elijah disgraced the prophets of Baal; the Bible says *and the fire of God feel and consumed the burned sacrifices and the wood , and the dust, and licked up the water that was in the trench.* **The fire of God is going to lick up every water spirit wherever they are, under the sea, Gods fire is going to lick them up and destroy them.**

Let's take time to pray; this was one of the hardest subjects to write due to the opposition, but I guarantee you, once you know the truth and exercise it you will see the victory. Let's disgrace this spirits; say this prayers our loud;

- ➢ Any witchcraft practice under any water against my life, receive immediate judgment of fire in the name of Jesus Christ
- ➢ Let every evil altar under the water upon which the devil is working against my life be destroyed by fire.
- ➢ Let the thunderbolts of God locate and destroy every marine spirit covens where decisions are being made concerning my lie.
- ➢ Any water spirit from my village or place of birth be amputated and destroyed by fire now in Jesus name.
- ➢ Any power of marine witchcraft holding my blessings be arrested by fire and recover all my belongings in Jesus name.
- ➢ Any spiritual spouse fashioned against me from the waters I break your covenant now in Jesus name, and declare I am no longer married to you.

- Every arrow projected against me from the sea; go back to the sender now in Jesus name.
- Every agent of marine witchcraft monitoring my progress be roasted now by fire in Jesus name.
- Every evil ever done against me by marine spirits and manipulations, be reversed now in Jesus name.
- Any evil contact points used in my body or house to manipulate me, I command them to be destroyed by fire in Jesus name.

THE CITY UNDER THE SEA

Before we go deeper I want you to read this testimony of Emmanuel Eli to expose the city under the sea and its operations.

'One evening, I decided to have a walk. Along Ebute Metta bus-stop, I saw a young beautiful lady standing. I never spoke a word to her. The next day while passing also I saw her still at the same spot. The third day I saw her still at the same spot and while passing she called me. I stopped and introduced myself to her as Emmanuel Amos but she refused to introduce herself.

I asked her name and address but she only laughed. She asked me mine and I told her the street ONLY. When I was about leaving, she said she would visit me one day. In my mind I said, that was impossible, I did not give her my house number how then could she come. But true to her words, I heard a knock on my door after a week of that meeting at the bus-stop. There she was, the mysterious lady! I welcomed her in my mind. (I wondered who this beautiful lady was, and did she know she was treading on dangerous grounds?) I entertained her and she left. After this first visit, her visits became regular without any relationships.

I noticed that in her visits she kept to a particular time, and would not come a minute earlier or later! In some of her visits I would take her to the Lagos Bar beach, or to the Paramount Hotel or Ambassador Hotel etc. All these while, she still did not tell me her name. I decided not to worry since I knew the relationship would not develop more than that. I had already been instructed never to touch a woman.

Suddenly she changed the day visits to nights. During one of the visits she told me: "Now it is time for you to visit me." We stayed together that night and at 8.00 a.m. the following day we took off. We joined a bus and she told the driver to stop at the bar beach. As we stopped, I asked her: "Where are we going?" She said: "Don't worry; you are going to know my house." She took me to a corner of the bar beach, used something like a belt and tied around us and immediately a force came from behind and pushed us into the sea. We started flying on the surface of the water and straight to the ocean. Dear reader, these happened in my physical form! At a point we sank into the sea bed and to my surprise I saw us walking along an express way. We moved into a city with a lot of people all very busy.

I saw laboratories, like science lab, designing lab, and a theatre. At the back of the city, I saw young beautiful girls and handsome young men. No old people. She introduced me to them and I was welcomed. She took me to places like "darkroom", "drying room", and "packing room". She then took me to a main factory and warehouse and then came to her private mansion. There she sat me and told me: "I am the **queen of the coast** and would like very much to work with you. I promise to give you wealth and all that go with it, protection and all that go with it, life and an 'angel' to guide you."

She pressed a button and a tray came out with human flesh (in pieces) in it and we ate together. She commanded a boa (snake) to appear and asked me to swallow it. I could not. She insisted but I could not, how could I swallow a live snake. She then used her powers and I swallowed it. These were three covenants: The **human flesh** and **blood, the snake** and the **demonic angel** were always there to make sure no secret was revealed.

But the 'angel' was given power to discipline me if I went astray and also to bring me food from the sea any time I was here on earth. I promised to obey her always. After this promise she took me to another part of the ocean, this time an island. There were trees and each of these trees had different duties:
- tree for poisoning,
- tree for killing,

- *tree for invoking, and*
- *tree for cure.*

She gave me powers to change to all kinds of sea animals like hippopotamus, snake and crocodile and then she vanished. I stayed in the sea for a week and through one of the means (as a crocodile) mentioned above I came back to the world.

The Underworld Laboratories

I stayed in Lagos for a week and went back to the sea, this time for two months. I went into the scientific laboratories to see what was happening. I saw psychiatrists and scientists all working very seriously. The work of these scientists is to design beautiful things like flashy cars, etc., latest weapons and to know the mystery of this world. If it were possible to know the pillar of the world they could have, but thank God, ONLY GOD KNOWS.

I moved into the designing room and there I saw many samples of cloth, perfumes and assorted types of cosmetic. All these things according to Lucifer are to distract men's attention from the Almighty God. I also saw different designs of electronics, computers and alarms. **There was also a T.V. from where they knew those who are born again Christians in the world. There you could see and differentiate those who are church goers and those who are real Christians.**

I then moved from the laboratories to the 'dark room' and 'drying room'. The dark room is where they kill any disobedient member. They kill by first draining the person's blood and then send the person to the machine room where he/she will be ground to powder and then send the dust to the 'sack room' where they will be bagged and kept for the native doctors to collect for their charms. There were more things which are hard to explain in writing. Despite all these powers in me, I was not yet qualified to meet with Lucifer but only qualified to be his agent. All the same I was satisfied that I now had powers and could face, challenge and destroy things at will. Could there be any other powers anywhere I mused within my mind.'

In 1990 a newspaper carried a story of some Russian scientists who caught a creature that was half human, half fish in the sea of Cuba. It told him that it was from a city under the sea and begged them seriously to be allowed to go. They promised to let it go if it told them a little bit about where it came from. It told them that it lived inside the water and occasionally came among human beings, mixed with them to pollute their lives. It then asked them to let it go, but if they refuse, it told them that a great misfortune and terrible calamity would befall Russia.

I grew up in a village where a lot of stories where told about mermaids and people disappearing into dams and rivers, I heard stories of snakes that lived in the sea, but there were all stories as it is with so many people today. Brothers and sisters in the Lord, there are marine spirits and there is a city under the sea, where the devil has his operational base.

The city under the sea is also in the Bible; Nahum 3:1-3 declares; *Woe to the bloody city! It is all full of lies and robbery its victims never departs.*

Listen to this Scripture in Ezekiel 26:19-20a; **For thus says the Lord God; When I shall make you a desolate city, like the cities that are not inhabited, when I bring the deep upon you, and great waters cover you. Then I will bring you down with those who descend into the pit.**

This is a world where people and their wealth are kept. Child of God this is the time for you and me to call upon God to bring destruction upon this wicked kingdom. The Lord is calling His church in these last days to take up their rightful place. The devil is defeated; it's up to the Church to put him where he belongs under our feet.

Every country, state, region, area, city, town, village, etc., have this marine evil spirits that is manipulating and influencing such a place and working in agreement with local witches, sangomas, wizards, Satanists and devil worshippers disguised as good members of society, some even pretending to be prophets or pastors.

In every 100 cases of divorce taking place worldwide, about 99% of them are caused or being manipulated by marine kingdom, evil forces. Marine kingdom is also responsible for the following problems affecting people:

- Road accidents
- Shortage of blood in one's body
- Bankruptcy and debts
- Unexplainable sudden loss of business
- Premature sudden death
- Chronic diseases
- Diabetes
- HIV and Aids (was designed in the kingdom of darkness.)
- Miscarriages
- Barrenness
- Eating or drinking in the dream
- Constant swimming in the dream,
- Demonic spiritual husband or wife
- Children problems
- Drug problems etc.

Marine spirits forces also seize people means of livelihood by storing them spiritually in their spiritual banks. There are people whose souls and spirits have been captured and imprisoned within the marine kingdom. You see them physically but they are not whole, meaning they are under demonic-spirit-control, that is controlling their body, but the real person of the spirit is gone.

Marine kingdom evil forces also use a lot of churches and pastors or leaders; they offer them spiritual powers to do miracles and to mislead multitudes. Be careful of water spirits; be careful of churches where they always use water or mediums or tangible things to take away the focus of people from God to objects or to man.

OUR FOREFATHERS AND WATER SPIRITS

I am second generation curse-breaker in my family, meaning my parents were saved and by the grace of God they broke a generational curse of disobedience. As far as I am told there were no born again Christians in my family, my forefathers were not worshipping God. There were trapped in demonic customs and embraced ancestors and not God. I am told they worshiped the elements and all kinds of things. Some had spiritual wives and husbands that were handed down from generation to generation. They honored the dead and worshipped the marine spirits. Most of our villages are named after these demonic names, with no meaning and life in them. When a child is born in my culture they put them in the rain, I believe this is form of initiation into the water spirits. We grew up with sea water in our homes and a background of demonic marine influence, but with no knowledge of it.

There is a strong link between ancestral spirits and water spirits. Most of our chiefs or kings are heavily involved in water spirits. That's why they are mostly immoral and have multiple women in their lives, because water spirits cause people to be polygamous and promiscuous. **Sexual sin is one of their altars.**

GENERAL FEATURES OF MARINE SPIRITS

1. **They cause sexual immorality**; (Pornography, homosexuality, same sex marriages etc.); any dream where you find yourself sleeping with someone, it's a spiritual spouse, a marine spirit and must be dealt with. All forms of sexual perversion come from the sea. They are all over the internet, media and promote sex. Sex is used by the devil because of its power to join the souls and spirits of men. Sex with spirits means you are one with them. Spiritual spouses are non-negotiable for born agains, they must be cast out at all cost.

2. **They control Wealth, innovations and governments**; well-known presidents and the rich people of this world, have sold their souls to the devil and are subject to marine spirits. They use the water spirits for power and control. Jezebel spirit, the spirit of control, manipulation and lust is also a product of the water spirits.

3.   **They control fashion, make-up and cosmetics**; a lot of hair products, cosmetics, fashion trends and technology are designed under the sea. We were once praying for a lady who was once in the sea, as we prayed for her, to my surprise she kept on pulling the braiding that was on her hair, until we decide to bring a scissor so she could cut the braiding fiber. Guess what? the more she got rid of the fiber, the more she was delivered. Ladies pray over everything you wear or put in your hair or body. The devil is using codes and these are things that give him access into our lives.

4.   **They cause accidents**; the devil worshipper's lives on blood, anyway they can get it, they will kill people on the roads for blood. They also work in hospitals and blood banks.

➢ **Every accident fashioned against you I bind and destroy its assignment in Jesus name; you will live and not die.**

5.   **They kill children or steal them**; most missing children and persons are taken by these spirits.

6.   **They promote new-age ideas**, demonic doctrines and destroy Churches; any plans to promote wrong ideas in our society comes from the sea. All plans to destroy pastors, families and Churches are planned in the sea. Most cults (so called Marine spirit churches) are products of water spirit.

7.   **They create diseases, miscarriages and defy the body**. They create demonic illness. Not all illnesses are normal. Satanists have confessed to having power to inject people with HIV and Aids, especially to the unbelievers and they did it without even touching their victim. They will greet someone and with their response the person will be infected.

'I declare every sickness from the kingdom of darkness that has been designed to destroy you. I cast it out of your body now in Jesus name. I command the fire of God to consume it and its senders. I declare you shall live and not die, to proclaim the glory of the Lord.'

'I declare God is going to shame all your enemies, and every assembly against your life will fall for your sake.

I declare by the Spirit of God, you will rise again and be healed of your infirmities, you will testify about this prayer in Jesus name.'

8. **They destroy marriages**; they are responsible for fights in marriages, unnecessary quarrels and misunderstandings, cheating and divorce. If there is one institution that the Devil hates, its marriage. The water spirits have chief demons that specialize in destroying marriages. They will try anything to make Gods holy marriage unholy.

9. **They responsible for financial difficulties**. You work like an elephant and reap like an ant. When you labor, but cannot see the harvest, know that there are powers at work.

10. **The sea is the glory swallower**; the glory of men and women even cities are swallowed in the sea(Ezekiel 27:27

SIGNS OF MARINE SPIRITS OPERATION

1. **Always swimming in the dream;** do you ever dream of always being in water or swimming, these could be a sign of connection with the marine spirits. Have you ever slept over a friend or a place and all you could dream was water; you probably were sleeping on a marine altar

2. **Snakes in the dream;** any involvement with snakes is a sign of marine powers at work. This dream should be dealt with. The devil possesses people with snakes, and even Christians if not careful can be possessed with snakes to bind them. **Any problems related with giving birth or barrenness is often a result of a serpent placed in the womb.**

3. **Crossing of rivers** with boat in the dream.

4. **Pride.**

5. Fear of rivers.

6. **Constant disappearance one's personal possession.**

7. Unusual Stubbornness.

8. **Easily irritated.**

9. **Unusual anger.**

10. **Thoughts of death or suicide.**

11. Wearing of ornaments whose sources one cannot explain.

12. **Sadness mood** without any cause.

MOTHER OF THE WATER (MAMNY WATER)

Ever heard of Mermaids, ever wondered if they were real? These are some of the spirit beings that reside in the water. The devil has disguised these spirits so well, that people think they are just a fairy tale and children love mermaids a lot. Mermaid spirit are called mother of the water, in Africa they are called queen of the water, or mother of the ocean. They rule over the seas, lakes and rivers. Mermaids are half human and half fish; they are demonic creatures that reside in the sea.

The most popular and powerful African Mermaid is named "Mamba Muntu" which is her personal African name. Mermaids possess inhuman beauty, unnaturally long hair of three different textures which ranges from straight, curly to kinky, and either black or blonde, and is combed straight back, and a high complexion that's beyond normal. Mermaids are popular for luring unsuspecting men into their seductive plan, they would lie on beaches disguised as woman, and once you attend to them, they can drown you or you come back possessed with special powers and would be used for her evil purpose. They have power to manifest as humans either man or female. Mermaids are said to possess wealth, jewelry, silver and gold.
Declare these prayers out loud;

- ➢ Any Mermaid sent from the underworld, against my life be roasted by fire now in Jesus name.
- ➢ I divorce myself from the mother of the waters in my family line. I renounce her I am not subject to her in Jesus name.

HOW DO PEOPLE GET POLLUTED BY MARINE SPIRITS

1. **Sexual sin**: All forms of sexual sin, will pollute you with marine spirits, lust, pornography, prostitution, polygamy, homosexuality and fornication are all used to pollute peoples spirits. Sleeping with a marine agent will make you one of them. Most prostitutes are marine agents.

2. **Ancestral and parental pollution**: This happens when your ancestors or parents are into marine worship. If you happen to come from a background of water spirits, even if you get saved, seek total deliverance in these areas.

3. **Environmental pollution**: When you live in areas surrounded by rivers or seas and you do not pray hard, you would get polluted too.

4. **Seeking fruit of the womb from the marine world**: Consulting the diviners or witch doctors or marine agents for having children, will immediately mean that child belongs to the devil and will be used, even sometimes to kill their parents.

5. **Family idols and altars**: What Idol or altar is your family founded upon. Many idol worshippers consult water spirits.

6. **Rituals and sacrifices**: A person gets polluted through these means. Have nothing to do with any rituals or ceremonies to honor the ancestors; do not be deceived into partaking or eating food sacrificed to idols. This will make you one with them.

7. **Direct attack through marine powers**: Sometimes this spirits attack families directly.

Pray this prayer now;

- ➢ In the name of Jesus Christ I cover my family and loved ones from any attacks from marine spirits, may the wall of fire be around them.

8. **Recruitment by gifts**: These powers have agents all over the world initiating people through gifts like money, cars, houses, jewelry, clothing, attachments, be careful of gifts, pray about anything that you receive.

9. **Parents that are marine agents**: Children born of such parents would be polluted.

10. **Initiation by friends**: If you have friends who are possessed with water spirit, they will initiate you easily through food, clothes, etc.

11. **Satanically inspired music and dance**: Many musicians get their inspiration from water spirits. Believers must be very careful. The way some dancers perform clearly indicates they are possessed by water spirits.

12. **Demonic movies and shows**: Be careful what you watch, the devil is all over the media and T.V. Children of God should be careful of this, especial for children as most of their cartoons are full of evil.

15. **Sharing cloths with marine agents**: Believers must be careful who they borrow things from. I will never forget one day we were in a home cell (house church), and a sister that was visiting us decided to take one of our born again leaders jacket, she wore her jacket without permission. I remember when we realized we drove back as we had forgotten it, and we found her wearing it. This was an agent from the marine kingdom sent to pollute our sister. We found her and the jacket, prayed over it and rebuked her for stealing.

16. **Food pollution**: Be careful where you eat. Even amongst friends or family. Be prayerful about your food and drink.

A person that has been polluted by marine powers would find it hard to serve God, because, this powers pollute the spirit of man. This information is not meant to scare you, but to empower you. Deliverance by fire and by force demands that we know what we are dealing with so that we can live in freedom, victroy and abundance.

FASTING AND PRAYER CHAPTER 6

This time I would like to urge you to take your prayer temperature to another level. The Lord is depending on your prayers. Not only for yourself, but for countless people out there that are bound.

For the next Seven days you going to fast and pray for total deliverance in this area. (This will be a water and juice fast, liquids only no food).

ROAD TO VICTORY FAST

DAY 1: Spend the day in repentance dedicate this fast to the Lord read Isaiah 58. Disconnect yourself from anything that might distract you.

- Make a list of people you need to forgive. And forgive them.
- If you have any items in your house that you are not comfortable with that are perhaps contact points, please get rid of them.
- If you have anything that you received from an ungodly source such as an herbalist, sangomas (witch doctors), physics or any such mediums. Get rid of it, if you can burn it during this fast.
- Seek guidance from your spiritual leadership, it may be a good idea to tell them what you fasting about, or at least to inform them you will be fasting.

DAY 2: Renunciation Prayers; Declare this prayers morning and night.

- I resign my involvement in any way to the marine spirits. I withdraw any part of my body and blood deposited on these altars in Jesus name.
- I withdraw my pictures, images and inner man from the altars in the sea and covens of evil association in Jesus name.
- I purge myself of all evil food or drink in my system from evil associations.
- I break all inherited covenants with water spirits.

- ➤ I renounce and divorce a spiritual husband/wife, I declare I am no longer yours, I belong to Christ and I break my covenant with you now in Jesus name.
- ➤ I break any soul ties with marine friends or associations.
- ➤ I claim back from Satan and all the marine kingdom, my earthly belongings in the custody of the spirit husband/wife

DAY 3-6: Battle of Midnight Prayers (these two to three days you will wake up at 12h00 in the night and pray these prayers)

'While men slept, his enemies came and sowed tares among the wheat, and went his way.' Matthew 13:25

This midnight prayers are targeted at scattering every programming of the devil through your dreams, every programming of the devil to the sun and moon against you.
Pray this prayers out loud, you can spend time on each prayer I recommend this prayers be accompanied by speaking in tongues if you can, pray for as long as you can, until you feel a release;

- ➤ All my stubborn enemies I command you to hear the word of the Lord now in Jesus name.
- ➤ Household marine witchcraft from the place of my birth, I command you to catch fire now and die in Jesus Name.
- ➤ Drinkers of blood, eaters of flesh I command you to perish in Jesus name.
- ➤ I disconnect myself from marine associations in Jesus name.
- ➤ Bondages of infirmity break in Jesus Name.
- ➤ Every mouth of darkness speaking against me, shut up and speak no more in Jesus name.
- ➤ Blood of Jesus wipe off every hand writing against my destiny.
- ➤ Communicating gadgets of darkness transferring my information catch fire now in Jesus name.
- ➤ You financial killer in my father's house, what are you wanting for die in Jesus name.
- ➤ Every good thing stolen from my life, come back now in Jesus name

- All my wealth stored under the sea, be rereleased by fire in Jesus name.
- Dragon withholding my wealth, I bind you now in Jesus name, and command Holy Ghost fire to destroy you and all your guards.
- Every witchcraft padlock bearing my name, lock up your owner in Jesus name.
- (Now touch your stomach or naval) I command every marine pollution to catch fire now in Jesus name. I vomit every marine demonic pollution now in Jesus name, **OUT of my body (X 7)**
- I flush my whole life, family, possession and destiny with the precious blood of Jesus.

DAY 7: Repeat day 3-6 and then at least three times a day pray these prayers at the end.
We know going to call down fire; this prayer is very powerful and the marine forces are going to leave you today;

- Call down the fire of the Holy Ghost(point your finger towards the direction of the sea, river or lake declare this prayers out loud at the top of your voice) and then for 21 times Call down Holy Ghost fire:

- Every spirit from the sea, I dismantle and frustrate your plans upon my life,
- Every place where my name is mentioned or written,
- Every contact material that you are using to monitor my life,
- Every spiritual husband/wife programmed against my life,
- **HOLY GHOST FIRE X21**

All this prayers are sealed with the precious Blood of Jesus Christ. Amen. Give thanks and praise His Holy name. May the Lord honor your faith, now that you are free, go and free others. Be blessed as you keep reading.

CHAPTER 7

DREAMS AND THEIR ASSIGNMENT

Dreams according to Gods plan were designed to convey a divine message from God to man via the supernatural. Job 33:15-16 explains this;

In a dream, in a vision of the night, when deep sleep falls upon men, while slumbering on their beds. Then He opens their ears of men, and seal instruction.

God designed you and me to have godly dreams, but Satan took advantage of this channel through the fall of man and brought corruption and manipulation. Matt 13:25; **while men slept his enemies came and sowed tares amongst the wheat and went his way.** The sole purpose of the devil is to sow destruction in people's lives through their dreams. He uses dreams to program man and to cage them. **Your dreams are your spiritual mirror.** I know for a fact that if I am dreaming bad or evil dreams I need to check myself spiritually. Sometimes they are just attacks, but the best way to monitor your walk of faith is to watch your dreams.

SOURCES OF DREAMS

1. From God; the plan of God is for you and me to hear from him in our dreams. There are certain instructions that God wants to give you, there are messages that he needs to communicate with you, and the best time to do that is in your sleep. Never under estimate the power of a dream, It was through a dream that Joseph became a prime minister of Egypt, despite all the bad things that took place along the way, but he held on to the dream God gave him. It was through a dream that God gave Solomon wisdom and riches; it was through a dream that God saved Jesus Christ from Herod when He spoke to Joseph. The Lord uses dreams to warn, instruct and direct our lives.

2. From the devil; the enemy hates you and me, and will use dreams to corrupt and manipulate man. Matthew 13:25 teaches us this; while men slept, his enemies came and sowed tares amongst the wheat. Note the Bible say his enemies, these were not outsiders but an in-house enemy, who knew exactly when to attack and how. The devil is a cunning creature, and knows exactly what to do. **All spiritual dream attack is tailor made for an individual. In other words you will dream what is relevant and specific to you.** The devil comes to kill, steal and destroy; we need to stand our ground. Every child of God need to know they not immune to dream attacks, but by the grace of God through prayer and covering the devil has no power to destroy your live. Declare this prayer with me;

> *Every dream pollution from the kingdom of darkness, I reverse it now in Jesus name.*

3. From the Soul and mind: Ecclesiastes 5:3 says; *for a dream comes through a multitude of business; and a fool's voice is known by multitude of words.* As you go about your lives events, you capture in your mind consciously or sub-consciously a lot of information. This information gets stored in your soul or mind, will and emotions. At night while you sleep these events play out in your mind, sometimes dreams are natural and mean no harm. You can dream about a good time you had with a friend or a long time memory. This dreams that do not carry any thread should still be placed under the blood of Jesus, but no need to worry about them.

TYPES OF DREAMS

Dreams will fall into these categories;
1. Instructive dreams; when God wants to give you a breakthrough sometimes he will give you an instructions. (Psalms 32:8)
2. Predictive dreams; there is no time or barriers in the spirit, God can show you the future through a dream. (Gen 41)
3. Corrective dream; God is a father who loves His children and sometimes we need to be corrected and showed the way. (1 Tim 3:16)
4. Warning dream; this is when God shows you danger before you get to it, sometimes he uses this dream to expose wrong associations.

5. Prophetic dreams; God reveals mysteries and prophetic messages through dreams.

CAUSES OF DEMONIC DREAMS

Demonic attack; sometimes the devil will attack you, for a mere fact that you are Gods child, there is war in the heavenlies to destroy you. I always encourage the saints to be militant, the Bible says we are in war, it actually calls us soldiers. So there will be attacks from time to time so the best way is to resist the devil and he will flee from you, as James says. Or in full it reads this way; *'Obey God, resist the devil, and he will flee from you'* (James 4:7) So, James is teaching us a two-part remedy. Firstly you obey God. Second, resist the devil.

> ➤ Every dream attack sent to drain your anointing; I command it to perish with its sender in Jesus name.

Family curse; unconfessed family curses bring demonic dreams and attacks. As a born again Christian it's very important that you go through deliverance from any family curses. When I was born again I still had dream attacks especially those of fear, I would be terrified in dream and subjected the spirit of fear. I remember I will dream of being in our house and suddenly the house will be pitch black with a demonic presence, it will be so terrifying that I will fight to get up. There was a bedroom of my parents that I could never get into. I had this dream for years even after being born again; I believe it was a family related curse, perhaps of the spirit of fear and torment. I prayed about it and one day I had this dream, and declared the word of the Lord that; I have not been given the spirit of fear, but of power love and the sound mind. It was the end of the torture, while in the dream I literally went into the dark evil presence, commanded it to go in Jesus name, I went into my parents room, which I had feared for years in this dream, when the spirit came to attack I remember shielding my whole family against it. It was a remarkable breakthrough, since then I never had it.

Possession of cursed items. Cursed items are contact points for demons. A preacher told a story of casting out a "demon of Karate" from a young man.

He had delivered him the previous year from the same spirit. The young man repented and quit karate. However, the demon manifested a year later in extreme outbursts of anger and displays of great strength. The root cause was that, he had kept his training gear and black belt displayed in a glass case in his room. Once these were discarded, and a second renunciation made, the man was set free. Watch out for demonic items, pictures or items. Anything that resembles satanic presence, get rid of it. Sometimes these cursed things are with our children, it might be a video game, piece of clothing. Cover your house with the blood of Jesus, and let your house be filled with godly items.

Wrong associations; Proverbs 13:20 "*He that walketh with wise men shall be wise: but a companion of fools shall be destroyed.*" There is power in fellowship and soul-ties can impact positively or negatively in ones live. I am very particular about who I befriend, there is no way you can walk with the fools and expect to be wise. **Show me your friends and I will show you who you are.** The Lord wants to free us from wrong associations, as born gain we are called to influence to be the salt and light of the world and not to be influenced. Be careful about wrong associations as the Lord, wants you to be wise.

Marine spirits; the marine kingdom is popular for recruiting people through dreams. I know a girl who dreamed of a man who offered her a chocolate in a dream and after she took it, she was told that tomorrow at such and such a time the man will come and then she will be taken somewhere. She agreed and guess what the following day the man came at the exact time as mentioned to her, and she was taken to the city under the sea, where she was slowly introduced into Satanism, promised wealth and riches for a her soul. She was there for the next 14 years of her life.

> ➤ **I declare every recruiting agent of darkness assigned over you and your household, be roasted now by fire in Jesus name.**

DREAM ROBBERS ATTACK

The devil is out to kill, steal and destroy; he is after your joy, blessings, health, family and ministry. You need to pray violently if you having repeated occurrences of the following;

- All forms of robbery attack in a dream, e.g. House break-in or snatching or car hijack.
- You dream of losing important documents, such as an Id.
- Nakedness and seeing your clothing removed from you.
- Living in house without roof.
- Losing money.
- Dreaming of lack etc.

Pray these prayers out loud;
- Evil arrows go back to your sender (x7)
- Holy Ghost fire consume every dream robber assigned over my life.
- (Hold your head) and apply the blood of Jesus Christ upon your mind in Jesus name.
- Every dream robber assigned to steal from me, I bind you in Jesus name and command you to perish in your ways.
- I command every stolen goods to be turned back to me in Jesus name.

LOSS OF SPIRITUAL APPETITE DREAM ATTACK

The devil also uses dreams to lower our spiritual appetite, watch out for the following dreams and pray accordingly:

- Eating heavy food.
- Sexual intercourse.
- Urinating uncontrollably.

Pray out Loud the following;
- All demonic caterers feeding me demonic food, I command you to catch fire and die in Jesus name.
- All injecting demons sent to poison me let your own poison destroy you in Jesus name.
- Arrows of infirmity sent into my body, I sent you back to your sender.

- In the name of Jesus by fire, by force I recover all my lost appetite for the things of God.
- I take back every miracle that belongs to me in Jesus name.

SPIRIT OF DEATH OR UNTIMELY DEATH DREAM ATTACK

Any death related dream is not good, and should not be entertained. The devil kills not only physically but spiritually. There are things God has deposited in you that should be born; there is an office in you that should be occupied. **Just as Herod wanted to kill Jesus at his infancy the devil knowing the office Jesus was going to occupy tried to stop him before his time**. Every spirit out there out to kill you before your time, I bind it in the mighty name of Jesus; you shall live and not die.

Some dream manifestations are;
- Seeing a grave.
- Seeing a coffin.
- Seeing being shot or stabbed to death.
- A relative sent into a mortuary.
- Singing burial songs.
- Falling unconsciously.

Read psalms 118:17, and pray aggressively the following;

- In the Name of Jesus spirit of death you shall not harvest my life (x7).
- Arrows of death you shall not locate me or my family in Jesus name.
- I break the covenant with death in Jesus name.
- I bind the spirit of the grave in Jesus name.
- Any dream of death I have ever heard, either of myself, my family or anyone connected to me, I declare you shall not prosper in Jesus name.
- Spirit of car accidents I declare you will not harvest my life.
- Infirmities and inherited life threatening diseases, you are not my portion in Jesus name.
- Cycles of pain and death, BREAK in the name of Jesus.
- Gates of death be shut upon my life and family in Jesus name.

- I will live long, and enjoy the fruits of my labor in Jesus name.

Note: as a born-again Christian you are not supposed to dream of dead people in any way. It's a demonic channel that the devil is using to introduce you to demonic practices such as psychics.

Pray this prayer and if needed take a 3 day fasting if the dreams still persist;
- Every door, spiritual eye or third eye opened to see the dead spirits; I command it to close now in Jesus name.
- Lord I will only see what the Holy Spirit wants me to see and not the evil spirits.
- I cancel every initiation declared upon my life that is a result of this dreams.
- I renounce every involvement with the dead in any way.
- I cleanse my dreams with the blood of Jesus and let go of any sorrow, guilt or ill feelings for the departed loved once.
- In Jesus name I receive deliverance in this area amen.

DEMOTING DREAMS ATTACK

The devil ultimately wants to shame you. He wants you to lose confidence in God; He wants you to be demoted so you can say there is no God,

Here are some dream manifestations;
- Seeing yourself doing a job below your standard.
- Seeing yourself in a small house.
- Seeing yourself being fired from work.
- Seeing people conspiring about your demotion.
- Seeing people plotting your demotion.
- Begging for money in dream.

Pray these strategic prayers;
- Any demoting household spirits I command you to bypass me in Jesus name.

- Arrows of shame and disgrace; what are you waiting for, back to the sender in Jesus name.
- I blot out with the blood of Jesus every demoting dream in Jesus name.
- Any garments of shame forced upon me, tear and catch fire now in Jesus name.
- Lord by your mercy, turn my demotion into promotion.
- Lord turn my shame to fame.
- Anointing of double honor, manifest in my life for all to see.
- Dream of rise and fall projected against me be destroyed by fire in Jesus name.

FAMILY CURSES DREAM ATTACK

The devil uses family curses sometimes to try and cage people, even Christians. Most of us come from backgrounds where our families or parents consulted mediums, familiar spirits and sangomas (witch doctors). You have accepted the Lord but never broke that generational curse, and in the spirit realm contracts speak. As long as that contract is still tied to your name you will have difficulties.

Some dream manifestations are;
- Seeing old dead relatives.
- Contracts that bear your name.
- Meetings where you are discussed.
- Evil items in your possession.

Strategic prayers are;
- Confess all known and unknown generational curse, cover everything under the Blood of Jesus.
- You arrows of generational curses break now in Jesus name.
- I command every evil spirit of generational curse in my life to be broken now in Jesus name.
- I release my destiny from any ancestral curse working against my destiny.
- All dead relatives, familiar spirits in my family I block your assignment in the name of Jesus.

FINANCIAL ROBBERS DREAM ATTACK

You labor a lot, but reap nothing; Haggai 1: 6, 8-9, 11. The Lord wants me to tell you that it's time to break free out of poverty, out of debts, out of financial limitations.

Dream manifestation may include;
- Putting money in your pocket, filled with holes.
- Being robbed of money in dream.
- Seeing yourself begging, in lack or destitute.
- Exchanging money in dream.

Confession and Repentance;
- Confess every disobedience and unfaithfulness in tithing and giving.

Pray;
- Spirit of poverty manifesting in my dreams I command you to be destroyed in Jesus name.
- Any curse that makes me to gather into a bag full of holes I cancel it now in the name of Jesus.

EVIL MONITIRING SPIRITS DREAM ATTACKS

You need to deal ruthlessly with evil monitoring spirits if you are experiencing the following;
- Seeing strange bird following you in the natural or in a dream.
- Seeing strange eyes in dream or natural.
- Seeing a fly following you.
- Hearing strange movements following you.
- Dreaming of a house without windows or doors.

Prayers;
- Any witchcraft satellite erected to monitor my progress, collapse in Jesus name.
- I destroy every in-house monitoring spirits, planted by the enemy in my house.

SPIRIT OF INFIRMITY (SICKNESS DREAM ATTACKS)

Have you ever gone to bed well and woke up sick, this is a sign of a dream attack;

Pray;
- Spirit of infirmity you are not my portion I bind you in Jesus name.
- Demonic sickness I command you to leave my body with all your possessions now in Jesus name.
- I break the spirit of sickness in Jesus name.
- By His stripes I am healed and delivered in Jesus name.

EVIL PATTERNS DREAM ATTACK

Yoke of evil family patterns is a uniform problem in a family linage; it is also called a yoke of collective captivity. **It is the battle your father or mother fought and is now facing you.**

Dream manifestation;
- Seeing yourself and your dead father/mother always together.
- Seeing yourself divorced.
- Seeing yourself back where you come from.
- Always late for meetings.

Pray;
- Yoke of collective captivity and non-achievement in my life break and release me in Jesus name.
- Yoke of collective captivity of no promotion and late graduation break and release me.
- I declare I am a curse breaker and I will not be bound by what bound my parents.

SPIRIT OF STAGNATION DREAM ATTACK

This is a terrible spirit, if the devil cannot stop you from getting to your promised land, he will delay you, just as he did with Israel In the wilderness. Deuteronomy 2: 1-3

Any dreams where you see the following;
- ➢ Going in circles, perhaps walking or driving.
- ➢ Seeing the same things over and over while you walk.
- ➢ Feeling caged, or limited.
- ➢ Your feet stuck in mud.

Pray;
- ➢ Spirit of stagnation, I command you to loose me and let me go.
- ➢ Any agent of darkness assigned to delay my breakthrough catch fire and die in Jesus name.
- ➢ I receive total deliverance from dream attacks in Jesus name.

HOW TO BREAK DEMONIC DREAMS

1. Close every evil open doors in your life, that are giving the enemy access into your life. For example you can remove gossip from your life, for example, if every time you hear some bad information on someone, you must insist on praying for them. The next time a gossiper stops you at your doorstep and has something to say, turn the gossip meeting into a prayer meeting "Oh, that devil sure is hitting our friend hard. Let's pray!" Start the prayer immediately. This is super effective!

2. Break unhealthy relationships. Your friends who are leading you astray must go. Those old friends who pull you down, they are a spiritual hindrance in your life, get rid of them.

3. Search your home for demonic icons remember anything that a demon would claim is unholy. Do these exercises prayerful as the Holy Spirit knows best and He will direct you.

'I pray that from today onwards that your dreams will be consecrated unto God, I apply the blood of Jesus upon them now. I decree divine visitation, prophetic dreams to be your lot. I prophecy elevation and

advancement upon your live. Every demotion is turned around to promotion. I prophecy health and breakthrough in Jesus name. May your dreams be filled with angelic activity, may you experience Gods divine instructions, guidance and revelation through your dreams. I believe God is heard your prayers. The name of the Lord be with you. Amen'

CHAPTER 8

DEALING WITH ALTARS & WITCHCRAFT ATTACKS

In this chapter, we are going to put an end to every altar that has altered your life. **God is going to raise an altar that is going to alter every altar that has ever altered your destiny.** Brethren in Christ we tired of negative altars that are speaking against us, this time around the Fire of God by force will remove them. The children of Israel had been prospering and walking in dominion. They were possessing their possessions and doing well. Then Balak hired an evil prophet Balaam to curse them! This prophet understanding spiritual things therefore prepared seven altars, the perfect altar. Seven is the number of perfection. When the prophet tried to curse God's people his altar did not work because sin was not found in the people of God. God had said to him in Numbers 22: 12; ***you shall not curse Gods people for they are blessed.*** This evil prophet did not give up. He prepared again the second altar seven times. This shows you that our enemy is very stubborn and does not give up.

What is an Altar?

- ➢ Altar is a place of spiritual sacrifice; it can be in the godly way or satanic way.
- ➢ It is a place of contact with the spirit world; altars are still used in the kingdom of darkness to make contact with demonic spirits.
- ➢ It is a place of communion with God or gods, whenever God wanted to establish covenant or speak to his servants He will require them to build an altar.
- ➢ It is a place of servicing and activating covenants; whenever demons or devil worshippers want to initiate or establish covenants they will use altars.
- ➢ It is an entry point of spirits into the earth; an altar serves as means of opening one to the spirit realm.

- It is the launching pad of spiritual operations to attack; when Balaam wanted to curse Israel he prepared seven altars to use them as a launching ground for spiritual attacks.
- It is a place of fellowship with the devil.
- Satanic altars are raised to stop people's progress; most breakthrough delays are by demonic altars blocking Gods intervention.
- They are raised to kill, destroy, and rule nations; great leaders of our world have altars where they draw powers from as they sacrifice on them.
- They are raised to stop the move of God; whenever Gods people are advancing the devil will build altars to try and block Gods move.

An underlying definition for altars is; a place of sacrifice for demonic agendas or service. As a child of God you need not fear, the Lord is going to put your enemies to shame, every altar is going to fall down and bow, God will never allow the enemy to win, let the Lord deal with demonic altars now in Jesus name, Pray out loud;

- Every altar raised against my life I command it to fall down by fire.

- Every curse projected against me from a demonic altar I scatter it now by fire.

- Holy Ghost Fire (x7) against every Balaam altar erected to curse my life. In Jesus name I pray.

DIFFERENT TYPES OF ALTARS

1. **Godly altars:** A child of God can raise an altar of prayer, intercession, worship, thanksgiving, tithing, sacrificial giving unto God and His kingdom. This counteracts satanic altars. I believe everyone should be part of this three altars under Godly altars, they are; 1) a personal altar, 2) a family altar and 3) a cooperate altar. Personal altar is your own personal quite time with the

Lord, family altar is for you and your family praying together, cooperate altar is for the church the saints where you gather for fellowship and worship.

2. **Marine altars**. The devil is set up marine altars in the land to service his operations in the sea. This are places located by the sea, churches that worship marine spirits all serve as altars for these spirits to be released into the earth. In the book of Exodus, God told Moses to go early in the morning to the River Nile before Pharaoh got there. This was so that he could cancel the marine altar that Pharaoh often sacrifices to.

3. **Territorial altars**. Every nation, town or community has its own territorial spirits that governs it, often these spirits are serviced through altars. The altars can be on the strongman of the city, a sangoma (witch doctor) or sometimes they located where satanic covens are operating, where people are sacrificed.

4. **Forest altars**: there are forests that are used as places of sacrifices.

5. **Road accident altars**: Road accidents are amongst many places where the devil has set up altars to sacrifice men, have you ever heard of a road where often accidents occur, it's all planned. We need to counteract these altars in the name of the Lord. Pray out loud;

> ➢ *I declare every Road accident altar set up against me, you will not harvest my life and my family and fellow men, and I nullify your power and destroy you by the blood of Jesus and the name of Jesus now.*

6. **The sun, moon, and stars**: The elements are a place where the devils operate; they can be used as evil altars and programmed to work against an individual. In Judges 5:20 we are told that the stars in their courses fought against Sisera. How can the stars fight? It was spiritual programming. Psalms 121:6 says; that the sun shall not smite you by day nor the moon by night.

In 2 Kings 3:26-27, the king of Moab offered his eldest son as a sacrifice to his evil altar and the Bible says those who fought against him departed from him and left to their home, Altars are powerful and I pray that God will open your eyes against evil altars, especially in your family confront them and destroy them.

WHAT ARE THE EFFECTS OF THIS ALTARS

- They cause open doors for evil spirits to move freely.

- Satanic altars oppose Gods will in families and people's lives.

- They are the reason there is endless struggles and suffering, crime, abortion and corruption in our land.

- They are the major cause of limitations and frustration.

- They delay the destiny of men.

- They are behind curses of divorce, poverty, barrenness, untimely death, etc.

WHAT IS THE WAY OUT?

1. **Genuine repentance**; If my people who are called by My Name, will humble themselves, pray and seek My face and turn from their evil ways, so will I hear from heaven, I will forgive their sin and heal their land (2 Chronicles 7:14). Unrepeated sin is a gateway for the devil to operate. The only reason the altar of Balaam did not work was because there was no iniquity found in Israel. We live in communities filled with violence and suffering, you can stand up against these altars, and repent on behalf of the land. God says in Ezekiel 22:30 *I sought for a man to stand in the gap before Me on behalf of the land, and I found none.* **God is looking for intercessors that carry His flame to confront these evil altars.**

2. **Spiritual warfare**; Luke 10:19 says *Behold, I give unto you power to tread on serpents and scorpions, and over all the power of the enemy: and nothing shall by any means hurt you.* You have the authority to destroy every demonic

altar, you have the power to bind every strongman, and you have the power to destroy gatekeepers. **Spiritual warfare is amongst the most powerful weapon given to Christian, with it you can change your life around, your family even nations.** When men violently combat demonic forces in the name of the Lord, when they use Gods council and wisdom, battle are won and destinies are changed.

3. **Raise and maintain a sustained altar of intercession until permanent victory is won**. There are some evil altars that require more than seven days fasting. Isaiah 62:6-7 says; *I have set watchmen upon thy walls, O Jerusalem, which shall never hold their peace day nor night: ye that make mention of the LORD, keep not silence, And give Him no rest, till He establish, and till He make Jerusalem a praise in the earth*. I have been in the house of prayer for 5 years and the Lord taught me so much about intercession. I am a firm believer in prayer, we are called to pray, and we are called to stand in the gap. God is calling the church to be a house of prayer for all nations.

4. **Service your altar continually with; fasting, regular prayers and the blood of Jesus**; I take communion daily to service my altar. In Revelations we are told that they overcame him by the blood of the Lamb and by the word of their testimony. Service your altar continually by sowing and giving in tithes and offering.

5. **Set the satanic altars ablaze by the fire of the Holy Ghost;** Use the prayer points in this book to confront these altars.

Here are a few prayer points to deal with evil altars; Begin with repentance and if possible take communion.

Pray;

- I renounce every connection with an evil altar and apply the blood of Jesus upon my life.

- Lord in the name of Jesus Christ, lift up your mighty hand and destroy every satanic altar, gatekeeper that fights against my finances and spiritual breakthrough.

- You strange witchcraft altar that is restricting my promotion, be destroyed now by fire in Jesus name.

- I release my name from every material that is serving as a point of contact from evil altars now by fire in Jesus name.

- I break and destroy every altar speaking against my progress.

- Every marine altar caging my life and possession, my marriage and children, I command you to catch fire now and scatter in Jesus name.

DEALING WITH THE SPIRIT OF WITCHCRAFT

Sprit of witchcraft is the spirit that seeks to manipulate and control your life. Witchcraft is listed amongst one of the works of the flesh contrasting the fruits of the spirit in Galatians chapter 5. It's the spiritual manipulation operating through the flesh, meaning through men, human agents. **As the Lord needs human vessels to perform His will on the earth, the devil uses witchcraft and possesses people to push his evil agenda**. There are at least four levels everyone should confront regarding the spirit of witchcraft;

1. The Sprit of Witchcraft itself.
2. The human beings possessed of devil to practice witchcraft.
3. The devices and weaponry of witchcraft.
4. The destruction of witchcraft that must be reversed or restored.

Read this Scriptures, before you go further: 1 Samuel 15:23, 2 Chronicle 33:6, Galatians 5:20, 2 Kings 9:22, Micah 5:12, Nahum 3:4.

Witchcraft was practiced in the Bible, both the old and the New Testament, even today this spirit is still in operation.

WHO IS PRACTICING WITCHCRAFT

Everyone is involved in one way or the other, either you are involved or have suffered the attacks and need restoration. Witchcraft affects individuals and families, if this spirit is not dealt with nations are at stake, families are at stake, **unlike marine spirit which is patient and subtle at performing their evil assignment, spirit of witchcraft is ruthless impatient and will seek to destroy its victims quickly**.

I want you to know that witchcraft is not only a spiritual force that is done by demons but humans agents are filled with these spirit and they practice this evil practice. Your enemy is the devil but we need to pray against these individuals that are enemies of God.

Ezekiel 11: 1-4,8 says: *Then the Spirit lifted me up and brought me to the East gate of the Lords house, which faces eastwards, and there at the door of the gate were twenty –five men, among whom I saw Jaazaniah the son of Azzur and Palatiah the son of Benaiah, princess among the people. And He said to me; ' Son of man these are the men who devices iniquity and give wicket counsel in the city, who say; the time is not near to build the houses; this city is a caldron, and we are the meat. Therefore prophecy against them…;….you have feared the sword, and I will bring the sword upon you, says the Lord.*

Witchcraft sprit is amongst men and woman, it's through people whom you might even know, just as Ezekiel could recognize these men, they had names and they were honorable men. Witchcraft is not amongst the old woman as we were taught, but it's amongst the honorable, those that community looks up to, the leaders of our time.

> - I pray that any human agent practicing witchcraft against you, be exposed and put to shame.

- I prophecy against their devices and weaponry projected against you and your family.

- I prophecy that their destruction will be reversed and that God will restore all that they have destroyed.

- I call upon Holy Ghost FIRE, upon every camp bearing your name, family, church or community. Let them be consumed in their wickedness in Jesus name.

As the spirit of the Lord lifts you up, may you see what the enemy is doing, may your level in the Spirit rise in Jesus name.

WITCHCRAFT IN THE CHURCH

Another important area that we should be careful of is the agents of witchcraft disguised to be men of God; **these spirits is known to perform magical miracles that deceive many into their evil doctrine**. The only way to discern this spirit is by prayer. There are so many churches and they all preach Christ and this can leave many Bible believing Christians confused, but there is a difference between the real Church of Jesus Christ and these so called churches. Look out for the following to be sure you are in the right church;

- By their fruits you will know them; what kind of fruit is your leader displaying.
- Is the church preaching the pure Gospel? If not don't stay there.
- Is the Church preaching miracles and not the miracle giver, God wants you to know Him and not miracles.
- Is the focus on soul winning or on miracles; most of this churches are always promoting miracles and not Christ and eternal life.
- Do they conduct an altar call; every true church should win souls by bringing them to the altar so they can be lead to the Lord.

- Are they selling water, oil or materials, be careful, Biblically speaking you should not put your trust in things, but in God.
- Who gets all the glory, the preacher or God, if it's to man leave that church.
- Is there a spirit of mammon, is the church always seeking money from people, if so be warned.
- Is there a lot of strife and immoral activity in the church; if so be warned.
- Is your leader a reputable man of God, what is their history, did they rebel from their former church, what about their household.
- Is there people being sacrificed, sudden deaths of members of the church.
- Is there holiness in the church, demons hate holiness?
- Is there liberty, is there true Love of God, is there a presence of God. The Holy spirit of the Living God.

Be prayerful as I said, the most important of all is your soul, make sure your leader is a preacher of the cross and of the death and resurrection of Jesus Christ, Make sure there is pure Bible preaching, Godly order and no funny things such as eating grass or sour milk. Jesus honors humans and will not humiliate anyone. **All prophecies that are coming towards you are to confirm what your spirit already knows**, be careful of people calling phone numbers and using divination to prophecy. God wants you to know great and unsearchable things you do not know, not the ones you know. **Prophecy is to edify, exhort and comfort and not to humiliate or bring people down.**

WHAT IS WITCRAFT ATTACK?

We have dealt with altars and the Lord lay in my heart strongly to deal with witchcraft attacks. I don't know how many people I know and have prayed for that have experience this level of attack. It's quite unbearable and if not dealt with can lead its victims even to suicide. The spiritual warfare attacks against you are often called witchcraft attacks

Witchcraft in this context is the spiritual force that Christians feel in their emotions, when under demonic attack. These kinds of spiritual

attacks can be like strong confusion, wanting to give up and quit, and depression.** They can be so intense that the victim even hears sounds or voices.

So where do they come from? There are people that release witchcraft arrows against you through the power of words or by controlling actions (or sacrifices). For example people filled with this witchcraft spirit against you, can do some sacrifices, or incantations, take a simple lock, mention your name and say, so and so I bind you through this padlock, then they lock it and within seconds the victim life is locked, perhaps you were due to get married, suddenly you can't or you were going to get a breakthrough, and things just got cancelled for no reason. **This spirit is a manipulating and controlling spirit; it separates its victims, draws their self-esteem and makes them feel miserable.** This is a witchcraft attack at work.

> ➢ Any witchcraft attack projected against you, back to the sender now in Jesus name.
> ➢ I reverse every incantation or words or actions that have been blocking your progress, by fire by force they must lose you now in Jesus name.

SUCKS LIFE OUT OF YOU

This spirit will wear you down; confusion is just part of the attack. This spirit is known to make people tired and extremely weak. Have you gone to work tired and came back tired, or gone on vacation tired and came back more tired. It's the spirit of heaviness or witchcraft. **The spirit of God is a life giving spirit, and the evil spirit does the opposite**. Once you are tired and weighed down this spirit can make you depressed. You tried vitamins, exercise but nothing works, it's a spiritual attack and needs a spiritual solution. Other victims will even literally feel sad for no reason. So next time you experience stress and unusual tiredness, know it's an attack and cast that spirit away.

MANIFESTATIONS OF THE SPIRIT OF WITCHCRAFT

- When you are in prayer and you suddenly feel weak, headaches or speechless.
- You get ill for no reason.
- You go visit someone and comeback weighed down or weak.
- You confronted a colleague or someone that was opposing you, then suddenly you sick.
- You feel tired when you shouldn't be.
- You happy today tomorrow you down.
- Your emotions are on a roller coaster.
- Suffer from depression.
- Have you experienced spiritual resistance?
- Feeling tired even to pray or read the Bible.
- Thoughts of suicide and quitting on life.

WATCH OUT FOR CONTROLLERS

Witchcraft agents will go out of their way to control and waste your time. It's not a natural thing, it's a spiritual thing. Scripture teaches us; *'Withdraw thy foot from thy neighbor's house; lest he be weary of thee, and so hate thee.'* (Proverbs 25:17).

Do you have people in your life that demands a lot of time from you, and often bombarded you with their stories, they control the conversation and after you spend long time with them you cannot even say what your meeting was all about, these are controllers they are used by these spirit to bring you down.

- Is there anyone who spends too much time with you either in person or on the telephone?
- Is there anyone who continually consumes your time, especially when you should be in church or busy with Gods things?
- Have you ever had a friend who wants to speak to you during a time of prayer or service in the church

Controllers operate in witchcraft often have no idea what they are doing. They seek to always associate themselves with people of high standing. They are glory seekers and like to be seen by everyone. May the

Lord expose such people in your life, so you know how the devil is using them.

Witchcraft must die prayer points;

Let's do some serious warfare now and claim your deliverance in Jesus name

(Pray these prayers aggressively with violence and prophetic movements such as throwing your hands and stamping your feet);

Exodus 22:18 says; Thou shall not suffer a witch to live.

- ➢ Every seat of witchcraft assigned against my life, receive the thunder of fire in Jesus name.
- ➢ Every strongman of witchcraft powers be pulled down by fire in Jesus name.
- ➢ Every network of witchcraft disintegrate now in Jesus name.
- ➢ Lord I scatter every assembly gathered at the gates to device destruction against me and my destiny; I command them to scatter now by fire in Jesus name.
- ➢ I reverse every witchcraft effect summoned against me in Jesus name.
- ➢ Every blessing held illegally by witchcraft powers be released now in Jesus name.
- ➢ Every vow, covenant of household witchcraft affecting me, be nullified now by the blood of Jesus.
- ➢ Every witchcraft padlock fashioned against my life, marriage and finances be destroyed now by fire in Jesus name.
- ➢ O Lord let my dreams and visions reject every witchcraft projection in Jesus name.
- ➢ Thank you Lord for answering my prayers. Amen

CHAPTER 9

RENOUCING MEMBERSHIP OF EVIL ASSOCIATIONS

This is a very short chapter , but one that will change your life, there is power in confession and renouncing, this prayer points should be said out load and they are for anyone who has been a member of any of the following evil associations;

- Traditional demonic rituals (honoring the dead believes and customs)
- Cults (any Church that does not preach pure Gospel)
- Marine rooted Churches that use water.
- Jezebel spirits (controlling, manipulating spirit)
- Marine spirits or water spirits agents.
- Covenants to spiritual spouse handed to you by parents or yourself.
- Evil family covenants that are void of Biblical principles.
- Churches that use water or evil objects or things that are idolized.
- Familiar spirits.
- Witches & Wizard.
- Satanists.
- Devil worshippers.
- Involved in false altars.
- Consulted witch doctors.
- Have had a false prophet lay hands on you.
- And all other occult societies.

CONFESSION: Col. 2:14, 2 Cor. 5:17.
I...............................AS A BORN AGAIN CHILD OF GOD, I STAND BEFORE THE LIVING GOD IN THE NAME OF JESUS CHRSIT MY LORD AND SAVIOUR, I RENOUNCE MY MEMBERSHIP TO ANY OF THESE EVIL ASSOCIATIONS (MENTION THE ONES THAT ARE RELEVENT TO YOU)

1. I reject, revoke and renounce my membership of any of the following evil associations: Jezebel spirits, Marine spirits, and Water spirits, Queen of the Coast, Mermaid spirits, Familiar spirits, Witches & Wizard, Spirit of Death and all other occult societies in Jesus Name.
2. I withdraw and cancel my name from their registers with the Blood of Jesus.
3. I reject, and renounce all such names given to me in any of the evil associations in Jesus name.
4. I resign my position in any of these associations and withdraw my services and responsibilities permanently in Jesus name.
5. I reject all the evil works I have done to innocent people through my membership with these evil associations and beg the Almighty God to forgive me and wash me clean with the Blood of Jesus.
6. I purge myself of all the evil food I had eaten in any of these evil associations with the Blood of Jesus.
7. I bind you jezebel spirits, Marine spirits, Water spits, Queen of the Coast, familiar spirits, Witches & Wizards, Spirit of dead, occult spirit operations in my life with hot chains and fetters of God and cast you out into the deep and seal you with unquenchable Fire of God.
8. I withdraw any part of my body and blood deposited on the evil altars.
9. I withdraw my pictures, images and inner-man from the altars and coven of evil associations.
10. I return to any of the evil associations I am connected with the instruments and any other properties at my disposal for the execution of duties.
11. I hereby confess total separation from the evil associations in Jesus name.
12. Holy Spirit, build a wall of fire round me that will completely make it impossible for these evil spirits to come to me again.
13. I break any covenant binding me with any of this evil association in Jesus name.
14. I break all inherited covenants and all such covenants; I consciously entered into in the name of Jesus.
15. I bind the demons attached to these covenants and cast them into the deep in Jesus name.

16. I resist every attempt to return me back to the evil associations with the blood of Jesus.
17. I renounce and revoke all the oaths I took while entering the evil associations.
18. I break and cancel every evil marks, incisions writings placed in my spirit and body as a result of my membership of the evil association with the blood of Jesus and purify my body, soul and spirit with the Holy Ghost fire.
19. I break all covenants inherited from my ancestors on the father and mother side in the name of Jesus.
20. Lord break down every evil foundation of my life rebuild a new one on Christ the Rock.
21. I command the fire of God to roast and burn to ashes every evil bird, snake or any other animal attached to my life by the evil associations.
22. I dismantle every hindrance, obstacle or blockage put in my way of progress by my involvement with the evil associations.
23. All the doors of blessings and breakthrough shut against me due to my involvement in these evil associations I command you open in Jesus name.

RENOUCING CURSES:

1. I break and cancel every inherited curse in Jesus name.
2. Lord remove from me all curses placed upon my ancestral families as a result of their evil associations' involvement.
3. I break and cancel every curse placed upon my parents.
4. I break and cancel every curse, spell, jinx, hypnosis, enchantment, bewitchment and incantations placed upon me by my involvement with evil associations.
5. I break and revoke every blood and soul-tie covenants and yokes attached to them.
6. I purge myself of the all the evil food I have eaten in the evil world with the blood of Jesus and purify myself with the fire of the Holy Ghost.
7. All demonic spirits attached to all these covenants and curses, be roasted with the fire of God.
8. I declare my body, soul; and spirit a no go area for all evil spirits.

DELIVERANCE PRAYER FROM SPIRIT HUSBAND OR WIVES:

1. Today I permanently divorce my spiritual husband/wife in Jesus name; I belong to Jesus and not to you.
2. I break all covenants entered into with the spirit husband or wife.
3. I command the thunder of God to burn to ashes the wedding gown, ring, photographs and all other materials used for the marriage.
4. I send the fire of God to burn to ashes the marriage certificate.
5. I break every blood soul-tie covenants with the spirit husband or wife.
6. I send the thunder of God burn to ashes the children born to the marriage.
7. I withdraw my blood sperm or any other part of my body deposited in the altar of the spirit husband or wife
8. I bind you the spirit husband or wife tormenting my life and earthly marriage with chains and fetters of God and cast you out of my life into the depth pit and command you not to ever come into my life again.
9. I return to you every of your property in my possession in the spirit world including the dowry and whatever was used for the marriage and covenants.
10. I drain myself of all evil materials deposited in my body as a result of our sexual relation with the blood of Jesus.
11. Lord, sent Holy Ghost fire into my root and burn out all unclean things deposited in it by the spirit husband or wife.
12. I break the head of snake deposited by the spirit husband or wife. To do me harm and command you to come out in Jesus name.
13. I purge out with the blood of Jesus every evil material deposited in my womb to prevent me from having children on earth.
14. Lord repair and restore every damage done to any part of my body and earthly marriage by the spirit husband or wife.
15. I reject and cancel every curse, evil pronouncement, spell, jinx, enchantment and incantations placed upon me by the spirit husband or wife.
16. I take back and possess all my earthly belongings in the custody of the spirit husband or wife.
17. I command the spirit husband or wife to permanently turn his back on me forever.
18. I renounce and reject the name given to me by the spirit husband or wife.
19. I hereby declare and confess that the Lord Jesus Christ is my husband till eternity.

20. I soak myself in the blood of Jesus and cancel the evil mark and writing placed on me.
21. I set myself free from the stronghold, power and bondage of the spirit husband or wife.
22. I paralyzed the remote controlling power and work used to destabilize my earthly marriage, hinder my child bearing for my earthly husband or wife.

COVENANTS AND YOKES BREAKING PRAYERS:

1. I break every evil covenant with water spirit and the yokes attached to it.
2. I break and cancel every covenant with any idol and the yokes attached to it.
3. I break and cancel any evil covenant entered into by my parents on my behalf and the yokes attached to it.
4. I commend the fire of God to roast the forces of hindrance and obstacles and paralyze the power in Jesus name.
5. Lord let the Holy Ghost effect immediate breakthrough in every areas of my life.

CHAPTER 10

POWER OF MIDNIGHT PRAYER

For years I have heard a lot of Christians speak about the power of praying in the night, I have heard it often said that; it's the best time and a lot of spiritual activity takes place this time. I can still remember attending my first all night prayer meeting and the expectations I heard. It was one of the most fulfilling experiences spiritually. I was never the same since. It brought so much hunger for the things of God, I believe that's one of the reasons I spend the next five years of my life in the house of prayer. I had discovered a secret to life, a secret to fellowship with heaven, a secret to walk with God and live in His presence. That secret was discovered in the quite night prayers, where I was alone with God. Have you ever longed to experience God in depth and quietness, I urge you to begin the midnight prayer. The power is not in the night hours, no! The power is in the Spirit of God in you who uses you in those crucial hours to destroy the plans of the enemy. **The kingdom of darkness is most active from these hours, it's active all the time, but the moment the clock hits 00H00 that's the time things are commanded and released into the spirit real to affect the natural.**

WHEN IS THIS HOUR?

Midnight hours are between 11.00pm and 3.00am in the morning. This is known to be the most spiritual active period of the night. Most dreams or visions from the Lord or evil spirits happen during this time. This is the time when the Lord ministers to you in your sleep, as I explained in the dreams chapter. The devil takes advantage of this time to plant evil things in man, to bewitch, to program all sorts of evil. Hence I believe every child of God is called to spiritual warfare we don't recommend that you sleep like everyone else. As the Spirit leads you, rise up, by the grace of God have regular time in the night to pray. It's the best time and all great generals in the faith did it. Jesus Himself prayed in the night.

THE POWER OF THE MIDNIGHT PRAYER

'And at midnight Paul and Silas prayed, and sang praises unto God: and the prisoners heard them. And suddenly there was a great earthquake, so that the foundations of the prison were shaken: and immediately all the doors were opened, and every one's bands were loosed (Acts 16:25 – 26). One of the most powerful spiritual tools that God has given to us, but so neglected by most Christians is the midnight prayer. Midnight prayer is the prayer done about 11pm to 3am. From the Bible and throughout the ages, the prayers done around this particular time have always brought great breakthroughs. As a Christian, it is imperative that you live a life of prayer.

A prayerless Christian is a powerless Christian.
Prayer is us giving God permission to intervene in our affairs.
Prayer is like a slender nerve that moves the Omnipotent hand of God.
The prayer of the night is the silent killer to every spirit that seeks your life.

God is calling us to a higher level. There are levels you can never attain in the spirit without mastering the act of praying in the midnight. There are revelations you will never get without prolonged midnight prayers. And there are also satanic powers, thrones and chains you can never dismantle unless through prolonged midnight battles.

BODY RESPONSE IN THE NIGHT

The human body is relaxed an unconscious during the night. Naturally, the body is always weak at this time of the night. And this makes it open to any spiritual manipulation. For one to be powerful in the spirit world, the person's human spirit must be guided and led by a higher Spirit, which in the case of a Christian is the Holy Spirit. And be so strong that the evil spirit will be repelled by your spirit.

WITCRAFT HOUR

Midnight is always a period of intense spiritual activities both by the Kingdom of God and the Kingdom of Satan. **If you want to be in charge of these activities around you and dismantle satanic plans in your life, then you must learn to wake up at midnight to fight against the powers of darkness**. For example, witches and wizards are very awake this time. These are agents of darkness possessed by the spirit of witchcraft. And these agents of darkness mostly operate in the midnight. Their assignment is usually to shoot their evil arrows or attacks at their victim, while their victim is asleep. And by the time the person wakes up, they will see everything going wrong. **This answers why people can be well one day and then after some weird dream they are never the same**. These arrows are meant to attack individuals, families, businesses, ministries, marriages and relationships, health, finances etc. Sometimes even peoples destinies are caged. A story I heard back home of an ex-Satanist was that; she was recruited in the night by a simple dream and one thing led to another until she literally left her body.

You may not believe this, but most of the problems we're going through today were first shot into our lives by demonic forces while we were sleeping (Matthew 13:25). **Do you know that almost everything about this life is decided in the spirit realm before they manifest physically?**
Whenever God wants to do something to you, to bless you or give you a breakthrough or word or vision that is to come to pass, He will in most cases reveal it in a dream or vision. The same goes for evil spirit or evil arrows they are first shot in the spirit realm before they manifest physically. Nothing happens just like that. **There is always a cause in the spirit realm, then the effect in the physical**. We must wake up and begin to control our midnights. This is where we have the battlefield. And our efforts here will determine how great, powerful, prosperous we will become in the daytime. It's called commanding the morning.

Job 38:12 puts it like this; *have you commanded the morning since your days began, and caused the dawn to know its place.*

You have the power to change the events of your life by commanding the day. **The Word in your mouth is like a seed, the new day dawning is like a womb; whatever you plant in it will come to pass.**

Command your Breakthrough now in Jesus name;

>1. Associations of wickedness gathered against my destiny, SCATTER BY FIRE!!! In the name of Jesus.
>2. Every wicked spirit against my prayer life, fall down by fire in Jesus name.
>3. My breakthrough is not negotiable, I move forward by fire!!! In the name of Jesus.
>4. The power that destroyed Goliath! The power that promoted Joseph!! Change my story by Fire!!! in the name of Jesus.

Declare this Scriptures now in Jesus name;

Psalm 119:62: *"At midnight I will rise to give thanks unto thee because of thy righteous judgments."*

Acts 16:25: *"And at midnight Paul and Silas prayed, and sang praises unto God: and the prisoners heard them."*

Job 4:20: *"They are destroyed from morning to evening: they perish forever without any regarding it."*

Exodus 11:4: *"And Moses said, Thus saith the LORD, About midnight will I go out into the midst of Egypt:"*

Exodus 12:29: *"And it came to pass, that at midnight the LORD smote all the firstborn in the land of Egypt, from the firstborn of Pharaoh that sat on his throne unto the firstborn of the captive that was in the dungeon; and all the firstborn of cattle. "*

Judges 16:3: *"And Samson lay till midnight, and arose at midnight, and took the doors of the gate of the city, and the two posts, and went away* *with them, bar and all, and put them upon his shoulders, and carried them up to the top of a hill that is before Hebron."*

Ruth 3:8: *"And it came to pass at midnight, that the man was afraid, and turned himself: and, behold, a woman lay at his feet.*

Matthew 25:6: *"And at midnight there was a cry made, Behold, the bridegroom cometh; go ye out to meet him."*

Darkness has binding powers, it limits lives activities. It has separating powers. At midnight that is when all that is evil and unworthy of light is let loose to those who do not know God; it's a time for wicked acts of evil. Your best friend can harm you at night without your knowledge. Most witchcraft meetings meet at covens at night. The spirit of a sleeping man is weak and harmless at night. Dream manipulators, night caterers, recruitment agents of darkness, terrible spirits are all active and do a lot of havoc at night.

You don't have to pray from 11am or from midnight to 3.00 a.m. Even if it is only for 15 minutes or 30 minutes, or 45 minutes, it is acceptable. Don't underestimate the power of midnight battles, it can desolate the camp of the enemy and obtain uncommon testimonies for you. The word of God prayed at midnight is the greatest force in the universe to be reckoned with.

START YOUR MIDNGHT PRAYERS TONIGHT WITH THIS POWERFUL DECLARATIONS; (Use most of the prayers in this book based on your need to pray in the midnight) Declare this prayers out loud;

1. Any power using the night to steal from me, be buried alive!!! In the name of Jesus.
2. Every night warfare that has prospered against me, die! In the name of Jesus.
3. Powers of the night assigned to disgrace me, I bury you now!!! In the name of Jesus.
4. Every satanic activity against me in the night be buried alive!!! In the name of Jesus.

5. Powers of the night troubling my dream life, scatter!!! In the name of Jesus.
6. Wicked mark put on my forehead in the night, be wiped off by the blood of Jesus, in the name of Jesus.
7. Every power blocking the way of my complete joy, scatter!!! In the name of Jesus.
8. Every power that does not want to let me go, be disgraced, in the name of Jesus.
9. Powers of the night troubling my habitation die!!! In the name of Jesus.
10. Every power searching for my face in demonic mirrors, your time is up! Die!!! In the name of Jesus.
11. Wickedness of the night assigned against my life, expire!!! In the name of Jesus.
12. Tonight, my Father, provoke Your violent angels to fight for me, in the name of Jesus.
13. Tonight, witchcraft bird flying against me shall die!!! In the name of Jesus.
14. Every enemy that came while I was sleeping, your time is up! Die! In the name of Jesus.
15. Pharaoh of my father's house, sink in the red sea, in the name of Jesus.
16. Anti-prosperity chains, my hand are not your candidate, break!!! Now in Jesus name.
17. Receive your deliverance and praise the Lord.

CHAPTER 11

MAINTAING YOUR DELIVERANCE

So now that you are free, you need to stay free by the grace of God. As Galatians 5:1 puts it; ***Stand fast therefore in the liberty (freedom) by which Christ has made you free, and do not be entangled again with a yoke of bondage.***

This shows you that a person can be made free and if they don't stand their ground, they will eventually fall again.

SEVEN STEPS TO MAINATAIN YOUR DELIVERANCE

1. **Put on the whole armor of God;** as set forth in Ephesians 6:10-18. There are seven pieces of armor: Make it a daily practice to put on the armor of God.

   - Your loins girt about with **truth**.
   - The breastplate of **righteousness**.
   - Feet shod with the preparation of the **Gospel of peace**.
   - The shield of **faith**.
   - The helmet of **salvation**.
   - The sword of the Spirit which is the **Word of God**.
   - **Praying in the Spirit.**

2. **Resist the thoughts that demons give you** and replace them with spiritual thoughts (Phil. 4:8).

3. **Positive Biblical confession** is faith. Negative confessions is demonic influence and will open the door to the enemy (Mark 11:23).

4. **Use Scripture;** Jesus withstood Satan's temptation by using Scriptures. Satan is not scared of your education or qualifications no! He trembles when you begin to quote the Word. The word is a two-edged sword (Heb. 4:12); and it is food for your spirit (I Pet. 2:2; Matt. 4:4). No one can maintain

deliverance apart from the Word of God as a primary factor in his or her life (Psalm 1:1-3).

5. **Take up your cross daily** and follow Jesus (Luke 9:23). If fleshly desires and lust of the eyes, are not brought to the cross, a way for demons to return will be left open (Gal. 5:19-21, 24). Commit yourself totally to Christ. Determine that every thought, word and action will reflect the very nature of Christ. Love, Faith and trust in God is the greatest weapon against the devil's lies (Eph. 6:16, 1 Corinthians 13).

6. Develop a life of **continuous fasting and prayer** which silences the enemy. Pray in the Spirit (in tongues) and also in understanding (I Cor. 14:14). **Pray without ceasing** (I Thess. 5:17).

7. Maintain a life of **fellowship with other believers, you must have a spiritual home and a spiritual father, you must submit to someone. This is very important**. It is the sheep that wanders from the flock that is most in danger. You cannot be all over the show, moving from church to church, you must have a home and that way you will be covered. Desire spiritual gifts and yield to their operation through you within the body of Christ (I Cor. 12:7-14).

HOW TO KEEP FREE FROM OPPRESSING SPIRITS

Have you ever been on the wild? If you wanted to sleep or camp outside you needed to make a fire, right! The purpose of this fire is to scare all the wild animals from coming to your camp. So it is in the spirit. If you want the demons to stay far away from you, simply be on fire for God. Be filled with the Holy Ghost and fire, be filled with the **Word of God** and be obedient to what the Word says.

You become God-possessed as you hear and do the Words of the Father. You become demon-possessed as you hear and do the words of the enemy (John 14:23).

- Avail yourself to the **Blood of Jesus**. Learn to ask forgiveness when you sin every time. Satan respects the blood (Rev. 12:11).
- Remember you are a son or a daughter and not a slave, God is your father.
- Take your freedom by **faith**. This is your position, declare it, stand on the Word, get stubborn with the devil, this is your heritage (Luke 10:19).

- **Resist the devil**, be sober and vigilant, resist the enemy steadfast in the faith, and he will flee from you (I Peter 5:8-10).
- **Love you neighbor;** Refuse to be hateful and mean; confess love (Matt. 5:44).
- **Forgive one another**; an unforgiving spirit lets the enemy on you again (Mark 11:25).
- You must **forsake sin** lest a worse thing come upon you (John 5:14).

HOLDING ON TO YOUR DELIVERANCE

1. **Focus your attention on Jesus** in everything you do (Rev. 12:11).
2. **Allow the Holy Ghost to have His way with you** (John 16:13).
3. **Immerse yourself in the Scriptures;** the Bible is the written Word of God (John 8:31).
4. **Tell the devil and his unclean spirits in Jesus' name to go away and leave you alone.** Make it clear that you intend to follow Jesus no matter what (James 4:7).
5. **Hang onto other Christians.** The Christian walk is not a one man walk (Gal. 6:2).

May the Holy Ghost uphold you as you stand your ground no matter what, the Word of God will always win, never give up on God, He will never give up on you!

CHAPTER 12

HOW DO I KNOW I NEED DELIVERANCE?

THE GIFT OF DISCERNMENT

To overcome demonic powers it is important to be able to recognize their presence and tactics. Thanks to God that the Holy Ghost has provided a special spiritual gift for this purpose. This gift is called **discerning of spirits** (1 Corinthians 12:10).

To discern means; to discover, evaluate, and make a distinction between what is right or wrong, evil or good.

The gift of discerning of spirits will enable you to discern the spirits operating in others. Not all spirits are of God, and the devil can disguise very well, this gift gives you permission to see that which is real or fake.

The gift of discerning of spirits is very important when dealing with demonic spirits. It enables you to immediately discern whether or not a person has an evil spirit operating through or against them. It takes away deception by seducing or lying spirits. **What demons say can be a lie**; do not depend on the evil spirit to inform you about their operation, but listen to God. Interviewing demons is not a good idea if you not having a gift of discernment you can be easily led astray.

When the Syrophenician woman came to Jesus with an appeal that He cast out an unclean spirit from her daughter, she said *"My daughter is grievously vexed with a devil "*(Matthew 15:22). How did she know this? She knew it by discernment and detection. Detection is simply observing what demonic spirits do to a person.

Demonic obsession and oppression; is seen by an unusual unfamiliar heaviness or obsession of some sort. To understand more on the differences between oppression and obsession read chapter 4.

Demonic obsession and oppression can be seen by the following signs:

1. **A physical binding**: The "daughter of Abraham" who Jesus healed of a spirit of infirmity was bound physically (Luke 13:10-17).

2. **Chronic sickness;** may be demonic oppression. Not all illness or sicknesses are caused by demonic powers. Some illnesses are caused by a violation of natural laws, such as not eating properly or drinking bad water. Some illness is also as a result sin. One king in the Bible who did not give glory to God was stricken with intestinal worms and died!

3. **Mental oppression:** unusual disturbances or confusion in the mind or thought life such as mental torment, doubt, loss of memory and many others. Restlessness, inability to reason or listen to others, abnormal talkativeness or reserve may be signs of mental oppression. All mental problems are not caused by Satan. Discouragement, depression, and disorientation can be caused by allergies to certain foods or a chemical imbalance in the brain.

God is able to heal mental problems and illnesses not caused by demonic spirits as well as bring deliverance in cases caused by spirits.

4. **Emotional problems:** Disturbances in the emotions which come and go, including resentment, hatred, anger, fear, rejection, self-pity, jealousy, depression, worry, insecurity, inferiority, etc. all this are signs of demonic oppression.

5. **Spiritual problems**: Extreme difficulties in overcoming sin, including sinful habits. Rejection of spiritual solutions to problems. Rejection of counselling or prayer is signs of demonic activity in your life.

6. **Financial and marital problems**; most marriages faces real life threatening challenges in their existence, but there are challenges that are very demonic as a result of witchcraft, marine spirits or spiritual spouses attacks. Anytime you and your spouse have issues that seems to separate you. Financial challenges that are unbearable, then know

that either you violating Gods principles of marriage and finances or you are under spiritual oppression.

Demonic possession can be seen by the following signs:

1. Indwelling of an unclean spirit: This is demonstrated by moral uncleanness and filthiness. It might include the desire to go without clothing. For examples see Mark 5:2 and Luke 8:27.

2. Unusual physical strength: A person shows strength beyond normal capabilities. For examples see Mark 5:3 and Luke 8:29.

3. Fits of rage: These fits may be accompanied by foaming at the mouth. See Mark 9:14-29 and Luke 8:26-39.

4. Changes in personality and/or voice: A person who is normally shy may become aggressive or violent. Actions as well as appearance may be affected. Moral character and intelligence may change. Voice may be altered. (See Mark 5:9.)

5. Self-inflicted physical injury: In Matthew 17:14-21 there is the story of a man's son who would cast himself in the fire. In Luke 8:26-39 this demon possessed man cut himself with stones to inflict physical injury.

6. Terrible anguish: Luke 8:28 means that this man went about crying because of the terrible inner torment caused by his possession.

7. Incapacity for normal living: This man could not live in society but lived in the tombs of the cemetery (Luke 8:27).

8. Obsessive immorality such as involvement with pornography, adultery, fornication, masturbation, homosexuality, and other sexual sins.

9. Strong compulsions toward eating disorders, suicide, self-mutilation, maiming and murder.

10. Addiction to drugs or alcohol etc.

11. Trances, visions, and meditation which are not focused on the one true God.

12. Bondage to emotions such as fear, anxiety, depression, hatred, rage, jealousy, backbiting, envy, pride, bitterness, negativism, and criticism.

And you shall know the truth and the truth shall set you free!

Have you been blessed by this book, remember to rate this book and sent a review on the book page in **www.Amazon.com**

For prayer requests or testimonies, sent us an email on **hlomph@hotmail.com**, we will love to hear from you.

May the grace of our Lord Jesus, the love of God and the fellowship of the Holy Spirit be with you now and always in Christ our Lord and Savior name I pray Amen.